A
Survival Guide
for those who have
PSYCHIC ABILITIES

•••••••••••••••••• AND ••••••••••••••••

DON'T KNOW WHAT TO DO WITH THEM

About the Author

Lisa Anne Rooney is a medium, life coach, and spiritual counselor who helps both the living and the dead move forward. She has been teaching psychic development classes for more than ten years. Visit her online at www.PurpleLotus66.com.

To Write the Author

If you wish to contact the author or would like more information about this book, please write to the author in care of Llewellyn Worldwide, and we will forward your request. Both the author and publisher appreciate hearing from you and learning of your enjoyment of this book and how it has helped you. Llewellyn Worldwide cannot guarantee that every letter written to the author can be answered, but all will be forwarded. Please write to:

Lisa Anne Rooney
℅ Llewellyn Worldwide
2143 Wooddale Drive
Woodbury, MN 55125-2989

Please enclose a self-addressed stamped envelope for reply,
or $1.00 to cover costs. If outside the USA, enclose
an international postal reply coupon.

A Survival Guide
for those who have
PSYCHIC ABILITIES

•••••••••••••••••••••• AND ••••••••••••••••••••••••

DON'T KNOW WHAT TO DO WITH THEM

Lisa Anne Rooney

Llewellyn Worldwide
Woodbury, Minnesota

FIRST EDITION
Third Printing, 2021

Book design by Bob Gaul
Cover design by Ellen Lawson

Llewellyn Publications is a registered trademark of Llewellyn Worldwide Ltd.

Library of Congress Cataloging-in-Publication Data
Names: Rooney, Lisa Anne, 1966- author.
Title: A survival guide for those who have psychic abilities and don't know what to do with them / Lisa Anne Rooney.
Description: First Edition. | Woodbury: Llewellyn Worldwide, Ltd., 2018.
Identifiers: LCCN 2018022815 (print) | LCCN 2018024721 (ebook) | ISBN 9780738756813 (ebook) | ISBN 9780738756516 (alk. paper)
Subjects: LCSH: Parapsychology. | Psychic ability.
Classification: LCC BF1031 (ebook) | LCC BF1031 .R6755 2018 (print) | DDC 133.8—dc23
LC record available at https://lccn.loc.gov/2018022815

Llewellyn Worldwide Ltd. does not participate in, endorse, or have any authority or responsibility concerning private business transactions between our authors and the public.

All mail addressed to the author is forwarded, but the publisher cannot, unless specifically instructed by the author, give out an address or phone number.

Any Internet references contained in this work are current at publication time, but the publisher cannot guarantee that a specific location will continue to be maintained. Please refer to the publisher's website for links to authors' websites and other sources.

Llewellyn Publications
A Division of Llewellyn Worldwide Ltd.
2143 Wooddale Drive
Woodbury, MN 55125-2989
www.llewellyn.com

Printed in the United States of America

Contents

Introduction

I stand at my front door watching my client walk to her car. As she turns to give me a small wave goodbye, I reassure her I will help her and tell her once more that I know everything will be better than okay. I step back into my house, close the front door, and take a deep cleansing breath ... it's only Wednesday morning and I've already met with nine people this week and seven of them are struggling the way I did in my past.

My name is Lisa Anne Rooney, and I am a medium. I see and talk to dead people. I can't remember a time I didn't see spirits, but it took me a *very* long time to accept and deal with my gifts, using them to enhance my life rather than cause constant struggle.

Every day I am reminded that I need to help these and many more people out there in the world who don't have a clue why they feel the way they do. These people usually don't know what is happening to them but know they feel off, or they have an idea what's going on but aren't sure how or if they can even connect to their abilities.

I have been doing sessions professionally for many years, and what I've learned is that I seemed to attract clients who are gifted but not using their abilities, just as I didn't. At some point, I realized that I needed to create a tool for them. My clients are the type of people who do not necessarily want to go join a spiritual group or church but realize that in order to be balanced, they must get a grip on their abilities. This is what ultimately led me to write this book. I fought my abilities and turned away from them as much as I could, but when I finally did start working on them and balanced myself, it changed my whole life. I am driven to help people and give them techniques and tools to use to connect to their abilities so they do not make the same mistakes I did.

There really are many reasons why I didn't realize it or believe I had special abilities, not in the least because I struggled with my reality of seeing and hearing dead people. One of the major reasons I struggled is the obvious—people would think I'm nuts! As a young child, I was terrified of the dead people I saw and didn't tell anyone what was happening because I knew people wouldn't believe me, and I also was raised Catholic where talking to the dead is a sin—"the devil's work." I thought it was best to suffer in silence, and as I grew up, my search became how to turn it off and control it. I was able to find a mentor, but to my surprise, lessons were more about honing my abilities, not shutting them off. But even with honing my abilities I still didn't see or understand the purpose of it all. Why should anyone be able to see the dead? What good is it? It's not like the spirits are here to give us lotto numbers (although maybe there are a few cases). Sometimes spirits have nothing to say but "Hello, I'm here" and when they do have messages, a majority of the time they are obscure, representing only a tiny piece of the whole puzzle of our lives. A lot of times, messages make no sense in the moment we receive them, but the good news is that Spirit often gives us messages we need to hear today in order to get to tomorrow … or a few days from now.

The craziest part for me is that I really only learned to balance myself through my unwillingness to accept my abilities. Without those struggles and lessons I learned along my journey to find a meaning to it all, I wouldn't be at a place in my life where I'm able to help others hone their abilities, balance their lives, and use their gifts to be able to empower themselves and be everything they want to be.

My goal with this book is to bring a different approach to the spiritual world through humor, fun techniques, and practices. I will show you how we all can be balanced— body, mind, and soul. In my struggle to stay normal and average, I learned that there is nothing normal or average about any of us. We are all extraordinary, if only we would just realize and believe it.

I'm a What?

I wake with a jump, my heart pounding and my eyes scanning my bedroom as quickly as I can. I see nothing that would have woken me with such a start. My eyes land on the digital clock on my bedside table, 3:15 am. I should have known, it's the witching hour, or as others call it, "dead time," between 3 and 4 am, the time when spirits, ghosts, and other paranormal things are said to be the most active. Honestly, I don't know if they are ever not active. Since I was a small child I have always woken up between those hours. It is strange, and I've always wondered why dead time is 3 to 4 am, but in all my research I have never discovered why, so who says it is the most active time? Probably people like me, the ones awake at 3 am. I flop back onto my back and lie in the dark, looking at the designs on the ceiling coming off the hall light. I listen to my husband's snoring and attempt to relax my senses. I would really love to be able to sleep through one night; I don't think that's asking much. I stare at the ceiling racking my brain trying to think about the last full night of sleep I had and quickly realize that I've never had one.

I take a deep cleansing breath, preparing myself to go through the mediation steps to relax my body and mind, allowing myself to hopefully fall back to sleep. Just as I close my eyes and start to relax the muscles in my feet I feel a poke in my ribs. I open my eyes, see nothing around me, and give up on sleeping for the moment. I climb out of bed and head to the washroom. As I sit down on the toilet I glance to my right; my breath hitches in my throat, a brief moment of fear rises in me, but I quickly suppress the fear and change it to an emotion closer to annoyance.

Standing in the dimly lit shower is a man. I growl to myself and curse my husband for not closing the shower curtain or swinging the bathroom door open completely to block the shower. I reach forward and try not to make eye contact with the man as I swing the door toward the shower so I can't see him. I'm exhausted and as I finish what I'm there to do I mumble to myself how I wish I had the kind of job that you left behind once your day was finished. My job is 24/7, and I can't turn it off, though lord knows there are times when I wish I could. This being one of them.

I stumble back to my bed, still mumbling to myself, hoping beyond all hope that I can fall asleep and not have any more disturbances. Just as I cuddle into my blankets, I feel yet again another sharp poke in my ribs. As I turn I finally see what or I should say who has been disturbing me tonight. An older gentleman with a shy smile, dressed in casual beige pants and a blue cardigan is standing beside my bed. It's the man I just saw standing in my shower. His energy gives me goose bumps up and down my arms, and the hallway light casts an eerie pattern on his face, making him look ominous and spooky. The energy coming off him tells me a different story, however; he is a kind spirit.

I roll over to face him. He isn't going to go away. I might as well see what he wants. I take a deep breath to prepare myself for another long sleepless night. I ask him in my mind how I can help him. I rarely speak out loud to spirits or ghosts because there is no need; and it is a good practice to have these conversations in your mind to stop you from speaking out loud. Trust me—when you're in the grocery store and a spirit comes up to you, the last thing you need is to be talking out loud to someone no one else can see!

It seems that this nice gentleman's granddaughter will be coming to meet me in the morning and he has a few words for her, and boy is she in for a lecture! I thank him for the early visit and tell him I will see him again when she arrives. He smiles at me, gives me a small bow, then turns and disappears in a shimmer. I breathe a sigh of relief that this visit was a short one. I turn, pulling up my covers and cozying into my pillow. I close my eyes and drift back to sleep, crossing my fingers that I only have one visitor tonight.

As much as I try to be normal and live a life like everyone else, my life is really far from it. There was a time when I worked really hard at separating my two sides, whom I called Lisa and Lisa Anne. Lisa is a wife, mother, and friend who goes to the park with the kids, walks the dog, and buys the groceries. Then there is Lisa Anne, the woman who sees and talks to dead people, feels energy from items and people, and who can look at a photo of a person and step into that person's energy to feel what is going on with and around them. My unwillingness to merge the two made my life a complete struggle. I was incredibly silly to think I could live as two separate people especially because one side enhances the other; separating them meant I would be unempowered and not my true self. Over the years, I learned to balance—how to use the Lisa Anne side to enhance rather than hinder my life and how my Lisa side enhances my Lisa Anne side.

My desire to stay grounded in this world and be "normal" (whatever that is) has taught me many lessons but chief among them is that it is possible to be able to be balanced. Although talking to ghosts and spirits is a huge part of my life, it isn't *all* of my life; I do not need to give up being Lisa in order to embrace my Lisa Anne side. In the past, I always held back because I didn't want to become what I call a spiritual extremist—someone who wants and tries to live their life only connected to the other plane, where spirits and other unknown things are said to exist. Maybe you know this kind of person, who only wants to talk about spiritual stuff and goes so far as to tie every conversation back to spirituality.

I often wonder why spiritual workers find it acceptable to preach to others every minute of every day. Yes, it is amazing to connect to the universe around us and can be a total high. I also know some people want to share that kind of passion with others (I do too), but there is a time and a place for everything. I do not want to talk about spirituality all the time and don't think it's healthy to do so. I can only imagine what the average person thinks about spiritual extremists. Imagine you have a friend who is a personal trainer and every time you get together, they stare at your body and talk about how to get fit and what you should and should not eat. This kind of person would make me want to go home and eat a double burger, not hit the gym! So when these spiritual zealots preach to people who are not interested in the subject, they actually turn them away from connecting to what could possibly make them whole. It is the furthest thing from empowering. The average person is not going to want to meditate or connect to their intuition or the spirits around them if they think they are going to turn into a spiritual extremist. The good news is that I know you can do all of that and still be normal, grounded in the material world.

Years ago when I started to throw around the idea of doing readings professionally, I struggled to understand why anyone would need or want to speak to loved ones who have passed. I understood that people who lost someone important to them needed closure and confirmation that their loved ones were still around and okay. But no matter what, it always seemed to me that I was missing an important piece of the puzzle to understanding my abilities and what I was supposed to do with them. I knew that people who went to mediums wanted confirmation or proof or were looking for a psychic, someone to tell them what their future holds. I am one but not the other—I do not see the future, I just talk to dead people. What spirits choose to tell me is all I can tell my clients, and if there is a bit of future info in the session, great, but if it is about the present, there is nothing I can do about it. I am a vessel or speaker for the dead people, and nothing else. My job is similar to that of an interpreter: the dead people tell me a message, I then pass on their messages.

Between trying to be an "average soccer mom" and not understanding the purpose in my abilities, learning how I fit into the spiritual world was difficult. As a result, over the years I've learned that as wonderful as my abilities are, they can also hinder me in my life. I am a humble person by nature, and I don't like to toot my own horn. When people would ask me if I was good at what I did, I would say, "I'm only as good as the dead person I'm talking to." I came to realize that's true to a point, but what makes me good at what I do is my ability and skill at interpreting dead people, which isn't always easy. Spirits and ghosts all communicate differently: some are straightforward (thank God), others show pictures and symbols, some give examples in my life to relate to my client's life, and some speak what I call "Yoda talk," like they are speaking in a cryptic manner that needs to be put together before the message is relayed. It took me many years to learn how to interpret spiritual messages. It requires patience (a quality I lacked but learned through honing my abilities) and practice.

I found that even after honing my abilities and analyzing how my sessions were unfolding, I still struggled with the reasons for a number of years until I realized that my sessions were more like life coaching with the dead people's help. Early on, when I was still trying to fit myself into that "medium" title (after all, I *do* see and talk to the dead), I had trouble because what I know now is that I do not fit that title perfectly. I was attempting to be a medium who dealt with grief and connecting living people with their dead loved ones, but readings always turned into being about the living, not the departed.

What ended up happening to me with the help of my clients and the dead people was that I realized I am here to teach and guide people to connect with themselves and their spirits with the help of the dead, *not* to confirm for my clients that their loved ones are around. It is more about the client than the dead people, the latter of whom are here to help us live in the now so we can realize our full potential and get that full life we all dream of. Spirit is always talking to me and my clients about the fact that there is no sense in living in the past or the future; the past is gone, the future just stays as the future if we don't do what needs to be done now or see the opportunities in front of us because we are too focused on the future or the past. Though we're human and can get stuck in life, the spirits can help us move forward. As the Dalai Lama said, "There are only two days in the year that nothing can be done: One is called *yesterday* and the other is *tomorrow*, so today is the right day to love, believe, do, and live."

I help and assist people living with grief in my sessions, but only a tiny bit is about remembering and confirming their loved ones are in the room with us. When those loved ones appear in a session, their messages are always about embracing life and living. In fact, the dead people have always told me that they wish we the living grieved for one day and then moved forward. I think that if anyone knows that life is to be lived, it is the dead. They want to be remembered and embraced, not pulled down with grief and sadness.

A normal session for me starts way before the client even arrives. Many times, like the story I told at the beginning of this chapter, a spirit arrives the night (if not days) before the client visits. As a result, my house can get very busy. I try my best to ignore the dead people until their living loved one actually arrives, but sometimes they are very persistent. Once I'm ready to connect, I sit down at my table, light some incense (usually frankincense—it's great for opening my third eye and also for protection from negativity), and say my prayers of protection (you will find them in this book). It is always a good practice to get into saying prayers when you are a medium. Approximately fifteen minutes before the client is to arrive, I open my aura and finally allow myself to scan the room for whoever is there to speak to the client coming. I greet the dead person or people, allowing myself to feel their energy and test out how they communicate. Doing so also allows me to have some control over how we communicate. Many spirits love to get close and their energy can affect me in strange ways. An example of this is times when I find myself scanning my kitchen and walls and the desire to clean becomes over-the-top strong, sometimes to the point where I find myself scrubbing the walls before the client gets there, only to confirm with my client that their loved one was indeed a clean freak!

Once the client arrives, I open myself to feel their energy. I can usually read peoples' energy very quickly, sensing nervousness, upset, excitement, confusion, and so on. Usually the energy flows from them like rays from the sun, allowing me to sink into my energy so I can feel what they are feeling. Depending on the energy, I gage how to proceed with the reading, always listening to what my guides and the client's loved ones are saying. I compare my inner dialogues with Spirit to being similar to a mom talking with a friend at coffee while her child is pulling on her sleeve and speaking at the same time as her friend. It's a skill that allows me to almost have multiple conversations at the same time, though I have to admit that no matter how hard I try to do this, there are times when Spirit wins and I lose focus on the living person conversation. People who know me tell me I get a "look" on my face when that happens … since I can't see my face I have no idea what the "look" is, all I know is I'm pulled for a brief moment into the spirit conversation and I can't listen to anything else.

I pull out my tarot cards and ask the client to shuffle the cards. This puts their energy onto the cards. I use tarot to focus myself and Spirit on the client's issues at hand. I then start the conversation fully with Spirit. I read tarot through Spirit and know the meaning of each card but allow them to tell their own story. Many times the spirits will get off topic and talk about another issue for the client but I try to get us back into the cards to stay on point. After the cards are read and the messages are given, I will look at photos of anyone living that they want to gather information about. I pass on what I can and then allow my clients to ask direct questions to their loved ones. I use dowsing rods for this part of the reading so my client can communicate directly without me having to deliver the message. The client asks a question out loud, and the spirits will move the rods I'm holding in a yes or no position in response. I love when the client speaks another language and still gets the answers they need while I simply act as the conduit for the energy to move the rods. Once my session is over, I thank my client and their loved ones on the other side for coming and escort them all out of my house. I learned early on that I had to tell the dead people to leave with the client; if I didn't, they would hang around afterwards wanting to talk more, causing me to have to call the client with further information.

My sessions with clients increased my belief that all of us have abilities—some people have gut instincts or intuition, and others have special sight or hearing that is turned up louder naturally. We can all hone what we have to enhance our lives. Imagine what life would be like if we actually learned to listen to gut instincts, moving forward through our fears and indecisions, seeing the opportunities and trusting them. I know all of you have been in the place where your gut told you to do something and out of fear or indecision you didn't go for it, then you had to live with the regret of not doing anything, watching as that opportunity passed you by. For some of us who have our universal speaker turned up louder than the average person, our abilities can actually hinder us emotionally and physically. A lot of people who are mediums or what some people in the spiritual world call sensitive (people who can feel energy or are connected to Spirit stronger than most) can experience anxiety, headaches, upset stomachs, and even confusion at times. So for a medium/ sensitive, it's not just about listening to our intuition and getting messages; that's a part of it, but not all of it. We must also balance ourselves so we can function day to day, and it is essential to hone our abilities and get a grip on them so they enhance us completely and don't make us want to lock the doors and never come out again.

Meeting clients who need help balancing led me to teach. I was blessed to meet my fabulous mentor, who changed my life and helped me realize that one of my purposes here in this life is to help and teach others. My classes are relaxed and there is zero pressure to perform, and I prefer a realistic, grounded approach. Everyone learns at different speeds for many reasons. We all have gifts but they are received differently. All classes start with a guided meditation, and in each session we focus on different ways to connect and receive messages, helping my students understand the feeling of connecting to the universe, Spirit, and their guides, in addition to how they receive messages individually. In the chapters that follow, I discuss techniques and helpful hints to help you, the reader, do the same thing at home.

Learning to connect to the universe and becoming aware of living in the now will change our lives and truly balance us all—body, mind, and soul.

2

The Early Years

To really know my journey, we need to go way back to when I was a child. My childhood was not easy, making this a hard chapter to write. Some of my first experiences with Spirit were as a child, and I have some wonderful memories among the dark ones. There was laughter and joy as well as times of struggle. From my experiences in childhood, I know that the sun is always shining, even when it is hiding behind the clouds. We should never lose hope, as things happen for a reason. I know I had to experience what I did so I could really understand some of my clients and also be able to teach my students who are struggling with their abilities to connect to Spirit. It is crystal clear to me now why everything happened the way it did, but in the moment I had no idea where it was leading.

Like many mediums I have spoken with, I used to live in a constant state of fear. The days were easier but the nights, not so much. I had difficulties sleeping, and was constantly bugged at night and terrified. Although the nights and spirits were many, I clearly remember a nice older lady often looking down at me. She seemed massive as she towered over my bed, but now I realize it is just that I was a child and she was an adult. I'm sure the fact that I was terrified also magnified everything. Her energy was kind and nice but that did not matter, I was not okay with her standing over my bed smiling at me. It truly terrified me.

Years later I found out who this woman was. We went to visit my favorite aunt and uncle, who lived in an old home in a small rural town in southern Ontario. The house was amazing—it had a huge wraparound porch and big windows to let in the summer sun. It was such a welcoming house, although I'm sure a lot of that feeling also had to do with the people who lived in it. I always felt warm, loved, and cherished in their home; it was a sanctuary for me for many years and a lot of my favorite childhood memories come from my time in their house. To this day when I smell that "older home" smell—you know, that smell of old wood and damp coming up from the basement—I'm transported back to my visits.

My love of old typewriters and writing come from my days with my aunt. I'd often pull out my aunt's amazing old typewriter. It was black with round keys (if I remember correctly it was a Remington), and it felt like it weighed a million pounds. I'd sit for hours practicing my typing skills and writing. One day while we were visiting, my aunt pulled out a large box from under the bed I slept in. I climbed down from the bed and sat on the floor beside her as she pulled the cover off the box. I peered in and was greeted by quite a few black and white photos. A little piece of my history sat on the floor in front of me and I was thrilled to dig in. I'd put my hand in and pull out a random photo and my aunt would tell me the details of the photo and fill me in on who the relative was. My family is large—my father had twelve siblings and my mother eight—so I was having a fabulous time hearing her stories until I pulled out a larger photo, an 8 x 10. When I flipped it over to see who or what was on it, I came face to face with the woman who haunted me many nights. My aunt took the photo from me, smiled, and then with a tear in her eye told me it was her mother. Grandma Le Clair stared at me from the photo. I had never met her in life, as she had passed away many years before I was even born, but I had heard a few stories of how strong and kind she was. My aunt gave me a hug and told me that she was sure Grandma Le Clair was always around, never far away. When I asked what she was like, my aunt laughed and said that Grandma Le Clair was a stubborn but loving woman and it would take more than death to keep her away from her kids and grandchildren. Boy, was she right about that! I had heard many stories about Grandma Le Clair but had never seen a photo until this day. Knowing that this was the woman who towered over me at night made it all so much more real. I wasn't crazy or imagining things, though at the time I wasn't sure if that was a good or bad thing.

In addition to Grandma Le Clair were other dead people and unknown energies that would get so close, almost nose to nose with me. I remember many times as a kid squeezing my eyes shut, knowing if I opened them, someone would be right there looking at me. But I couldn't help it, I'd open my eyes and only a few inches from my face would be a smiling dead person. Talk about horror movie scary! To this day the one thing that drives me crazy about dead people (besides them showing up in my bathroom) is that dead people really do not know or appreciate personal space.

As a child, I always attempted to get into my parents' bed at night, believing in the safety of numbers. I laugh now when I think back to how I handled it. I would lie awake with my eyes closed knowing that if I opened them I'd see something or someone I didn't want to see. When I finally built up the nerve to get out of bed and head to my parents' bedroom, I would quickly stand on my bed and leap out of my room into the hallway. I didn't really want to walk past or through the dead people in my room. I was so terrified that when my parents finally got angry and laid down some ground rules, I'd still sneak in to their room and lie on the floor at the end of their bed. It was horrible and exhausting, never mind extremely uncomfortable.

I never told anyone the truth about why I was so terri-fied, often using the excuse that it was my older brother's fault for teasing me constantly and telling me that Big Foot lived under my bed. It seemed like a crazy story, but the truth was even crazier. At the time, I was convinced I was cursed or evil, and it seemed better to lie. In a Roman Catholic upbringing, it is a huge sin to see or talk to dead people, or so I thought. As I got older, I realized it is necromancy that is considered a sin, which is invoking the dead. It could be argued that I do invite them when I do my sessions, but honestly I've never had to invite a dead person—they just show up.

Seeing spirits was the secret of all secrets to me, so as a child I had a ton of secrets for a while. Another one is that my father was always away "fishing" or "working"; what I didn't know then was that he was having affairs and leaving my lonely mother to raise us and take care of our home. My mother was a wonderful woman and I was always very connected to her. I loved her and wished that she could see what I saw: a woman with caramel-colored hair and eyes as blue as the clearest day in summer. She took care of her children as best as she could and baked amazing bread. She loved her children fiercely. One of my favorite memories of my childhood with my mother was what she'd do for us after we came in from playing in the snow. She'd make us hot chocolate and open the stove door, placing a blanket over the door. She'd pull three chairs in front of the door and my brothers and I would sit drinking our hot chocolate with our feet resting on the door, warming them from the heat coming out of the stove. Her love for us was always there, even in her darkest days.

Unfortunately, she didn't realize for a long time what a strong and amazing woman she was, only calling herself weak. It took a major shake-up for her to finally connect to her strength. When I was around eight or nine years old, my mother started to drink heavily; by the time I was ten, she was a full-blown alcoholic. This was also the time that my dad's secret came out. Dad left, and my mother spiraled further and further into the bottle. The next few years were lived in constant fear. I honestly don't know how I did it. I would get up, having slept only a few hours, constantly bugged by the dead people. I'd leave to go to school and on returning had no idea what I'd find. Was my mother sober, drunk and lying in a pool of vomit in the kitchen, or dead? I remember clearly walking home with my friends from school and chatting, but when I'd reach my driveway, my pretend life at school would slip away and my fear and real life would return every step up the driveway. Then night would come and my fear would only increase until sunrise, and the process would start all over again.

I do know that a few things got me through this time: my friends, music, and my roller skates. At home, I'd lock myself in my room and listen to music, which was (I now realize) a form of meditation. I would put my headphones on and the real world would drift away, and I'd be within the music, calming me and allowing me to have the strength and ability to deal with another night and day. It also allowed me to shut the dead people out. I couldn't hear them when Genesis was singing about ripples never coming back or the trick of the tail in my ears. I could just close my eyes and ignore that I could feel the dead people moving around me.

When I was around thirteen, my mother finally got sober. What led to my mother getting sober was hitting rock-bottom, as is common. One afternoon, I was in the kitchen on the phone with a friend when my mother, upset at something or someone, came into the kitchen to "get a coffee," which was really whisky in a mug so we'd think it was coffee. (She wasn't fooling anyone but herself, especially when you could hear the tinkle of ice hitting the sides of the mug as she drank.) As my mother left the room, a spirit came up the basement stairs straight toward me. I was frozen with fear. The woman was older with curly gray hair and a huge amount of energy coming off of her. I remember her clothes like it just happened yesterday: her top was white with small blue flowers all over it and she had a blue skirt with a frilly apron over it. She came nose to nose with me and told me my mother had just taken a bottle of pills and was going to attempt to kill herself. The woman told me it wasn't time and I needed to do something about it.

This was one of the first times I can clearly remember a spirit communicating to me. Though I'm sure they tried multiple times, my awesome ignoring skills prevented me from hearing them. This woman, however, didn't give me a chance to ignore her—she stood nose to nose with me until I hung up on my friend; I'm not even sure if I made an excuse, told her the truth, or just hung up. I was completely freaked out by this dead woman's confrontation. When I turned around after hanging up the phone, the woman was gone.

I went upstairs and found my mother asleep in her bed. I was not sure what to do. I laid down beside her and figured if she was going to die, I wanted to be there with her. I loved her and didn't want her to die alone. I was terrified and sad and started to cry, which was rare—I'm not a crier but couldn't stop myself. She woke up and asked me why I was crying. I told her I knew what she had done and didn't want her to die. She sat up, looked at me in a daze, and got out of bed. I was not sure what to do next; all I knew is I just wanted this to stop. She walked out of the room and headed into the bathroom. I curled up on her bed, trying to decide what I could do. Should I call 911? A neighbor? I prayed as hard as I could that she would live. A few minutes later, I heard retching sounds coming from the bathroom—my mother was making herself throw up the pills. That night when she did finally go to sleep, I spent that entire time checking that she was still breathing.

I didn't see the dead woman again, but that night as I paced the hallway, a sense of calm and knowing that it was going to be okay came over me. The next day my dad showed up with a friend who was a recovering alcoholic and they talked to my mother. She started Alcoholics Anonymous that night.

You would think that after this experience with this dead woman whose message basically saved my mother's life, I would change my attitude toward the dead people. You'd think I would have learned to listen to them … but I didn't. It took me many more years to actually listen to— not just hear—the dead people and their messages.

Time went on and my life started to improve. I started high school. My mother became sober and started to work again. For the next four years we had our ups and downs; my mother would fall off the wagon but get right back on. I enjoyed school socially but was a closed book to most people. I joke now that I was well balanced—I had a chip on *both* shoulders. I was a brooding teen but having a huge secret made it tougher, so I became quiet and angry, really skilled at ignoring the dead people during the day. I honed my no eye contact rule and for the most part it worked. The energy of other students and teachers affected me while at school, but if I had music and was able to go outside, it helped.

This was also the time in my life when I started to realize that organized religion was not for me. I always felt that there was more, that one religion has only a tiny piece of the whole. I started to read about other religions and faiths around the world. What I read fascinated me, but I still stuck with my Catholic faith even though I doubted most of the dogma. Religion class was very interesting for the rest of the kids as a result. I drove the nuns nuts asking my questions, constantly pushing. I wasn't anti-Catholic, only

anti-dogma. I wanted to know "why" other than "because."
"Why" quickly became my favorite word.

One of my favorite teachers at the time was a nun who
didn't wear a habit; she was in an order that wore all gray.
Sister Michelle was a tiny but fiery little woman. She coached
the soccer team and was the coolest nun I've ever met. We
had some major debates in class, on the soccer field, and
any place we ran into each other. She often got frustrated
with me because she couldn't answer my questions to my
satisfaction. Sometimes, if not most times, there weren't any
answers to religion questions other than "because that's the
rules." I respect Sister Michelle's commitment to her faith,
and I think she enjoyed my reasoning and the psychology
behind it all. I understand faith, belief, and trust, but there
has to be a sensible reason to it all.

I understand now that some people need religion to
guide them and it works for them, which is fabulous. Ultimately, I believe people should think for themselves and
learn to truly connect to God, the Universe, an unnamed
higher power, Allah, Buddha, Krishna, Brahma, Jehovah,
Jah, Ik Onkar, or whatever name you want to put on the
higher power/universal power. I think religion or spiritual
practices should enhance us, empower us, make us better
people, and assist us to do just that. It should not weigh us
down in fear, rules, and judgment of ourselves and others.
Some of us do not fit into any form of organized religion,
whether that is a mainstream religion or a spiritual church.

Some of us just connect to the universe in different ways. And as an adult, after pushing away from organized religion because of my belief that rules and dogma are crazy, I came to realize and accept years later that some people need it, and for them it is a wonderful thing.

My family's lives started to become full around this time, so I was left more and more on my own. My mother started to work shifts. The nights my mother worked and I didn't have the security in numbers factor, I would completely panic. When the night started to fall, I'd sprint through the house, turning on every single light—and I mean every light, even the stove. I'd push a chair into a corner of the living room and sit there for hours until someone came home. It makes me giggle now to think of how silly I was, but I had no clue how to deal with the dead people or even if it was possible. When people would ask why I would light up my house like a beacon, I'd just lie and say I was afraid of being robbed, which was a lie because we lived in a really nice neighborhood. At this point I had somewhat shut off the seeing, or thought I had. But I could still feel the dead people very strongly. I knew where they were and when they were moving around. I could sense them getting closer to me and I could feel them watching me.

What I found out years later is that in reality, I was really making the situation worse. I tell this to the students I teach now. We need to remove the fear. The dead people need energy to manifest. The only more powerful energy than fear is happiness and laughter, meaning that the amount of energy that comes off us when we are afraid is huge. Think of the movie *Monsters Inc.*, in which monsters came out of kids' closets to scare them and harness that fear energy for use in their world, giving them power and energy to function. It is the same with dead people, spirits, or ghosts—they need energy to manifest in the physical as well as to talk with or guide us.

Not only was I using huge amounts of physical energy (the lights), I was also beyond terrified that I was sending out huge amounts of my energy to the spirits. I knew that most dead people are here to help us, so I was afraid dead people would come in to "help" me. I dreaded nights because I could sense the spirits and then more would come in to help, making me even more afraid, and you can see where this is going. My fear was causing havoc in my life, bringing in more of what I feared.

When helping people who are sensitive to the dead, the very first thing I teach is the importance of removing the fear. Sure, I still get a moment of adrenaline when I walk into my bathroom in the middle of the night and a man is standing in my shower, but I push it away quickly and take control. It is a must when dealing with the dead, whether it is a ghost or spirit. But especially when it is a ghost. There are a few reasons why we shouldn't go into fear, which I discuss in a later chapter, but the main one is control: when dealing with ghosts we need to show them who is in control.

At the end of high school, I can't say I was upset or going to miss everyone. I knew the majority of my classmates were going to stay in my life for a while, especially because they needed me to counsel them. I thought I'd finally gotten to a point in my life where I could be free to live the way I wanted to. Boy, was I wrong.

Although my childhood was darker than some, I would not change a thing about it. I have some wonderful memories mixed with the chaos and tough lessons, and it all molded me into the person I am today. My experiences give me a perspective some people may never have, so I'm grateful and blessed to be able to have that.

.... **3** ....

I'm an Adult ...
Now What?

My parents had agreed in their divorce that when I turned eighteen, they would sell our house. I was really mixed up by this news because although I had sleepless nights and strange feelings in the house, it was what I knew. I had been dealing with those energies my whole life; even though I still ignored them, they became familiar. What would happen when I moved somewhere else? The thought terrified me. I didn't realize then that spirits can follow or visit the living wherever we are, as they are not trapped in places. Some ghosts can be trapped, but a lot of them can travel as well. My Grandma Le Clair and my other loved ones would find me no matter where I was.

The first place we moved into was an old house converted into apartments. It was in an area of town that had large old trees with branches that hung over the streets, and it was very quaint for being in the middle of a large steel town—in fact the area I was in almost didn't fit in with the rest of it. The house sort of had an *Amityville Horror* look to it, but once you stepped into the house all that changed—the couple who owned the property had gutted it completely. Everything was new and updated. My bedroom was in the basement, and although that room was old and creepy, it had fabulous energy and I felt completely at home there. I don't know if it was because of the remodel or the house was just a really happy one, but I loved it. Unfortunately, my time there wouldn't be for very long; the owner decided to move in, so my mother and I had to move on.

Although we didn't move very far from the quaint neighborhood, it was enough of a change that we went from quaint and quiet to the hustle and bustle of the city. We moved in an apartment in a large apartment building that was fairly new but haunted. Despite our past, my mother and I had always been close, and we functioned with a level of respect. I often think this is because I had always felt like I was the mother in our relationship; I'm sure in a past life I probably was her mother, and maybe everything we went through with her drinking was karma and paying a debt from a past life.

Although we were close and could speak about any-thing with each other, dead people was one thing we never discussed. There were definitely moments—especially when we moved into that apartment—when my mother tried to start up a conversation with me about it. I'd be sitting at the kitchen table eating breakfast and she'd walk in and ask, "Did you hear me scream last night?" I would look at her over my mug of tea and always answering the same way: "Nope." She would sit down and look me in the eye and say, "I woke up in the middle of the night and a woman was standing beside my bed. I screamed and then she disappeared." I would shrug my shoulders and finish my breakfast. Other times, my mother (who loved to read) would hand me a novel and say to me, "You should read this. It's a really good story." I would start reading the book and quickly discover it was about ghosts.

Thinking back, it could've been that my mother was trying to tell me about herself or trying to get me to confess my secret to her. I'm sure it was both. After she died, I was contacted by many of my cousins on social media, and a few of us noticed a link between us. Many of us are connected to the paranormal/spiritual world in different ways. We shared stories about our mothers and had similar stories—all our mothers at some point commented on seeing spirits or ghosts, yet none of us had an open conversation about it. Our mothers' reluctance to bring up the topic has a lot to do with religion as well as the era they grew up in, which was not as open as it is now.

I did my best to make excuses or not make a big deal out of what was happening, and for the most part it was easy for me to walk around my mother's little hints about spirits, at least until our apartment became party central for ghosts. The over-the-top activity started about a year after we moved into the apartment. The first time, my mother and I were coming back from grocery shopping. As we entered our apartment, I could feel a different energy in the house. I couldn't say anything to my mother of course, but I didn't have to—as we started walking down the hallway toward the kitchen with our bags, my mother started to freak out. She was not one to freak out, so I knew something major was happening. She dropped her grocery bags and started pointing at the pictures on the wall. I approached her and looked where she was pointing... every picture with exception of one or two very large ones were hanging upside down.

We went through the whole apartment and found that along with the pictures, some of the ornaments had been moved: some were facing backwards, some were bunched together. I knew it was dead people who had done it, but I convinced my mother that someone was playing a joke on us. I firmly said that the superintendent whom my mother was friendly with must have come in and was messing with us. My excuse worked for a few days, until my mother ran into him and he promised he was not responsible. He also told her that other people were reporting similar strange occurrences as well. She came rushing in with this news, so I brushed it off and told her there was nothing to be done. Even if we were being haunted, what were we going to do? We needed to live with the fact and move on. Meanwhile I was freaking out inside, I had no clue how to deal with any of this.

The activity carried on for about a year; nothing seemed to happen while we were in the apartment, only while we were out. There were a few occasions when something did happen during the night, but I'd quickly readjust the pictures and ornaments so my mother never knew. Every once in a while I'd still try the "it's not a dead person, Mom, it has to be someone coming in and messing around with us." She would always look at me like I had three heads and say "Lisa, if someone was coming into our apartment when we are not in, they would be stealing from us, not rearranging our ornaments and pictures." She had a point but I stuck with my denial game.

I never saw the dead person who was playing games with us but I felt the energy—it was feminine and a bit on the unstable side, which worried me but I never once felt in danger. She was more or less mischievous and that only made me anxious because I was always in a state of waiting to see what she'd do next. However, the chaos left as it came; it just stopped one day, which was okay by me, but every once in a while I'd think about her and wonder where she came from and where she went. My best guess is that she came in with someone who moved into the building and left with them when they moved out. Wherever she is now, I hope she has crossed over and has found peace.

Over the next few years, I did the things a lot of us do: I worked, met my future husband, Steve, and married him. Many strange and weird things happened over the years that threw me off balance but years later I've realized they taught me a lot of things, especially that ignoring my gifts does not work. I traveled a bit with my husband and had an amazing residual energy experience in Scotland (see chapter 7). On that trip, I understood what residual energy was and how lucky I am to be able to feel and work within it.

My husband had a huge career change in our late twenties; he went back to school and the next few years was centered around traveling and gaining experience for his career. This change sent us all over North America, but one part of our travels stands out: the Canadian Rocky Mountains was an experience that led me to have no choice but to deal with the dead. Banff Springs Hotel and Chateau Lake Louise in Banff National Park, Alberta, are two of the most haunted places I have ever been. In fact, Banff Springs Hotel is so haunted that the Canadian Mint has released a collector's coin featuring a depiction of one of the infamous ghosts that haunt that hotel. So many people have witnessed this ghost, who is named "the Bride," that it is not a legend, it is a fact.

My husband and I both got jobs at Chateau Lake Louise, a magnificent resort hotel situated approximately 6,000 feet above sea level among the mountains in Banff National Park. When our orientation began, I quickly realized that this was not going to be the average work experience I was expecting it to be. This was my first time being in a place where ghosts were freely talked about. During the weeklong orientation, we were told about the many ghosts inhabiting the hotel, certain rooms and experiences others have had, and the history behind them. The discussion was required and brought up in a casual manner (openly talked about as fact, not fiction) so that new employees would not freak out. The staff even gave us hints about how to react when confronted by these ghosts. I have to say, it is one of the first places where I have ever experienced others' first-hand stories. Normally when we hear about others' ghost experiences, it is almost like an urban legend or fifty people removed before you ever hear it. Chateau Lake Louise was different—most of the staff had firsthand experiences.

My first shift at the hotel was at night, and it ended up being an extremely exciting experience, which made up for the horrible uniforms we had to wear (think nightmare Swiss Alps: a full skirt with a burgundy blazer, a beige frilled shirt with Swiss designs down the front, and a rosebud bow tie. I cringe just typing it out.) At first, all I had to do was deal with questions and helping guests settle in, but as the evening wore on, guests tucked themselves into the cozy beds and the energy in the hotel started to calm, going from a whirling energy to a soft hum. Working this shift was myself and another woman who had been working at the hotel for a year or so to train me. She taught me how to complete the day's paperwork and how to set things up for the next day. Once we completed our work we were able to sit and enjoy the splendor of the hotel lobby, which was massive. The area in front of the reception desk has large arched windows and doors. The mezzanine level looked down over the lobby with a balcony surrounding it. A giant Swiss-themed chandelier hangs in the middle of the room, and the detail on it is unbelievable. You could stare at it for days and still not see every detail.

There were moments when I could feel a dead person walking by or watching us, but I kept my head down and my focus on my coworker. Around 1 am, we were at the front desk listening to security officers on walkie-talkies as they made their rounds. All of a sudden, one security officer started screaming at the top of her lungs. She had opened the closet on a floor where it's said that a maid can be seen hanging from the ceiling, and sure enough she opened the door and saw the ghost. We were told during our orientation that this door was *never* to be closed, as that's when the ghost maid appears. This poor security guard flew down the hall of the floor she was on, into the elevator, through the lobby, and out the door. She never returned. I asked the other security guard the next night if she was okay and if he had heard from her. Apparently, she refused to return even to pick up her belongings—she wanted them shipped home. This guard had been at the hotel for a couple of years and was quite relaxed about the whole thing. He smiled at me and said, "Yeah, she was a non-believer. I guess she believes now." He laughed and walked away. I do not think there was one day that went by without someone having a run-in with a spirit or ghost.

Although many deaths happen at the hotel (and indeed, normal hotels see their share of deaths), a lot of people unfortunately have heart attacks or other medical emergencies there due to its elevation. The hotel's history is full of tragedy with multiple fires and deaths, but the energy in the hotel was for me a nice, comforting buzz; nothing evil or twisted surrounded this hotel. I don't know if it was the fact that if I did slip up and say something about seeing ghosts no one would even bat an eye, or if it was that I was becoming more comfortable with the dead people, but I was not as frightened. Night shifts were better in this way because the living human energy was low and the hotel was a quiet, peaceful hum. I was allowed time to really see and feel the spirits and the residual energy.

One night, we all experienced the thrill of a lifetime. The weather had not been great that day, and the wind started to pick up as the sun set. Before we knew it, heavy rain was falling in sheets. I love thunder and lightning storms but this storm was a storm I would not forget for many reasons. The energy was buzzing inside the hotel and out. You could almost taste the warning that something was about to happen.

As the storm became more severe, more and more guests flocked to the lobby to watch Mother Nature in rare form from behind the massive arched windows. It was a show of a lifetime. Lightning was striking the earth, cracking trees in half. The floor to ceiling windows shook from the force of the thunder. We had no choice but to sit in wonder at this display... at least until everything went pitch black. I have experienced darkness before, but being 6000 feet up on a mountain, surrounded by the largest mountain range in Canada, is something else; it is so dark that you cannot see your hand in front of your face. Normally the only light at nighttime is the moon and the many stars (there are so many that it seems unbelievable it is the same sky you would see from the city). This night, the clouds covered both, so there was absolutely no light from the skies to illuminate the area. We waited for the generators to kick in, and there was a moment of pure silence before the guests started getting restless in the lobby. With the help of the security staff and their flashlights, the staff scrambled to get things in order. We located our flashlights and candles and started to walk around calming the guests the best we could. The lightning and thunder show that was fascinating only moments before became a threat, and each boom and flash was a show of terrible strength and power that clearly told us mere humans who exactly was in charge in the wilderness. After twenty minutes or so, we were informed by maintenance that a tree had been hit that not only took out the power lines but had also crushed the generators. The hotel would be in darkness until the hydro workers could get the main power back on. There was no hope for the generator, it had gone to generator heaven.

The staff started the long process of walking each guest up to their rooms, but even then, some staff members refused to assist the guests—they were not willing to be alone in the dark in the stairwells or some of the floors. Personally, I couldn't wait to escort the guests! It was a thrill to be on these floors knowing that at any moment, I could come face to face with one of the infamous ghosts with only a candle to light my way. As the guests dispersed, I noticed the energy adjust. The living human energy was calming down but the fear that was hanging in the air was giving the ghosts more energy. I'm sure the electricity in the air from the lightning also added even more for the ghosts. It was the strongest I had ever felt the ghosts and spirits up to that point. I escorted the last guest up to their room, and on my descent down the stairs, I felt as if someone was behind me. I glanced over my shoulder, bringing the candle to reflect toward where I just came from, but didn't hear or see anything.

As I continued down the stairs, I could hear breathing behind me. I stopped again and looked to see if someone was messing with me, but there was no one to be seen. Now my pace quickened as I started down again, and the breathing became louder and I could now feel a presence behind me! Well I didn't stop this time—I knew it was a ghost or spirit, and my former excitement of running into one vanished and was replaced with fear. I spoke to the spirit/ghost, telling it to back off and please let me get out of the stairwell safely, but I did not receive any reply. I'm not sure if that was because I was still in a place in my life where although I was opening up, I was still afraid. A lot of beginner students are like this, wanting to talk to Spirit or receive messages but also being reluctant and stuck in a place of fear. Although I may not have really wanted to hear from the spirit behind me, I was not completely afraid of it; I was more afraid of my candle going out and having to feel my way down the stairwell.

It took until the next afternoon for the power to return. I have to admit I was a bit disappointed; I wanted another evening of darkness so I could explore a bit further with a couple of the other staff members.

My husband had a firsthand experience with a ghost and didn't even realize it until it was over. He was working alone when he heard amazing piano music coming from the dining room. He came out of the kitchen to investigate where the music was coming from, and when he entered the large dining room overlooking the Victoria Glacier, he found a young girl at the piano in the restaurant playing. His first thought was, "Wow, she is an amazing player considering how young she is." As he came farther out into the dining room, she looked over at him and he spoke briefly with her. When he went back in to the kitchen, the playing stopped. He came back out to make sure she closed the dining room doors when he realized the doors were chained; no one could have possibly come in through those doors. The only other way to get in and out of the dining room was through the kitchen, and he was in there so he would have seen her walking past. She had just disappeared.

When I told others about his experience, they all laughed and said, "Oh yes, that's the concert pianist ghost." They told me about how a few years prior, the night manager received multiple calls from the guests one evening, complaining that they were being disturbed by loud piano music coming from the restaurant. He went to the floor to see what was happening. When he walked off the elevator, he could hear the most beautiful music coming out of the restaurant. He walked in and found a young teenaged girl sitting playing the piano. He asked her what she was doing playing so late. She told him that her parents had taken her to dinner that night in the restaurant and she saw the piano. She couldn't sleep, so she came back to play it. He informed her that it was too late and he needed to ask her to stop and go back to her room. She was very nice about it. He told her he would walk her back to her room. He turned away, heading toward the door, when he realized that she wasn't following him. He turned back to where she was sitting but she was gone— she had just disappeared.

People often hear piano music playing, and the staff will just head up to the restaurant and ask her to kindly stop. She does so, only to return a few nights later to play again. When I told my husband, he was utterly shocked. What took him most by surprise besides the fact he spoke to a ghost was that this girl was completely solid, not what you normally hear about ghosts. She did not have an apparition-like appearance; she was as solid as you and me, he said.

Besides the night of the storm, my personal experiences all involved a service elevator in the kitchen. There is a little boy ghost who plays with this elevator. You get in and press 11, and he will take you to every floor except the one you want to go to. People have reported that when the doors open on any given floor they see him standing in front of the elevator doors looking straight at them giggling. Then the doors close and you are whisked to another floor where he may or may not be standing. Other people report that sometimes the doors open and he won't be there, making you feel relieved ... but then as the doors start to close he'll stick his head into the opening, giggling because he tricked you. It was fun for him, like peek-a-boo. Any time I'd have to use this elevator and I could feel his presence, I would tell him off as soon as I got in the elevator. He would take me to a couple different floors but eventually, after putting my foot down, he would know I was not happy with him or going to play with him. He'd give up and take me to my floor. I have to say it wasn't my instincts that told me how to handle him, it was the other staff members who taught me what to do after I complained about the elevator having a mind of its own.

Though I have many stories from the hotel, what was most important was that being there allowed me to work and feel comfortable, gaining confidence with my abilities. I could let go of a bit of the fear and open up more to see-ing and hearing the ghosts as well as speaking openly about feeling or seeing them to others. My husband and I only spent a few months in Lake Louise before heading to our next destination, but for me what I remember most was connecting to ghosts, not just spirits, and realizing the big difference between the two.

When we finally ended up in Atlanta, Georgia, I found myself surrounded by really open-minded people who would constantly talk about ghosts and spirits, and/or people who were very interested in alternative spiritual practices. I worked as a production coordinator for a production company that filmed TV commercials and food shows. One of the newer pilots the executive producer and director decided to work on was a show all about spiritual practices. The first pilot was about astral traveling, so during filming I found myself in a studio with a handful of extremely interesting people. I'm a huge believer in the idea that everything happens for a reason, and this was one of those cases. Working in the film industry led me to working with people who practiced and used their abilities to enhance their lives, something I didn't even know was possible.

The pilot episode included a rocket scientist at NASA, an ER surgeon, dowsers, mediums, and an expert on astral travel from the Monroe Institute. All these people from different walks of life all experienced astral travel. They had science backing their experiences as well as their own stories, of course. In between takes, I'd pull as much information as I could from these fascinating people. In particular, the most interesting to me were the rocket scientist and the surgeon, two people who lived and breathed science yet were firm believers in the unknown.

The scientist talked a lot about crystals with me. He told me that as a scientist, he knows and uses quartz to run certain kinds of equipment. He held up his watch and said it was a watch with quartz movement, run by a small crystal inside. He explained to me that humans only know a small amount about what and how much energy is within crystals, so he wanted to help me look further into using them. It was fascinating, and I have attempted to work with crystals a few times but to me they are similar to drinking—when I hold certain crystals, the energy makes me lose control and I don't like that at all.

The surgeon had much to say; he told me that he had proof that a certain part of our brain is used to communicate with the dead. Someone like a medium has no choice in the matter, he believed, because that area is open and some people cannot turn it off or shut it down. He also said he believes that a lot of people come off unstable because of that, usually seen as people who talk to themselves or react to things that aren't there. His belief is that those people are talking to the other side but have no idea how to control it, and thus it has taken over their lives. Speaking from personal experience, I thought he was right—I could easily walk around talking to dead people all the time, and actually I do but not out loud. And there *are* times when I make faces at the dead people talking to me and receive the odd strange look from people passing by.

My time working at the production company was also when my abilities started to get stronger and stronger. I was having a hard time ignoring the dead people, seeing them everywhere. My no-eye-contact technique didn't seem to work any longer, and I wasn't sure who was dead or alive. As a result, my anxiety skyrocketed. I was afraid to go out, especially to highly populated places. I could feel energy coming off of people and places to the point that I didn't know what was my feelings or someone or something else's. I was getting information on people I didn't want to get. I was still unsure what to do, or even if anything could be done.

Around this time, I became pregnant with my daughter. I thought my abilities were increasing before, but I had no idea how out of control they would become! After she was born, the terrorist attacks of September 11th happened, so we decided to head back to Canada to be around family. The production company I was with was also going through a huge transition.

Once we were on Canadian soil, I felt lost and without a clue as to how I could move forward with life. I was having issues with my eyesight, headaches, upset stomachs, and anxiety. One day my husband suggested I go see a psychic because the traditional doctors were not coming up with anything. I found one psychic, a wonderful British lady who told me I needed to hone my abilities; she said I was out of control and she could teach me. This was the first developmental meditation class I ever attended and halfway through the class I knew I had found what I was lacking. It was just that this class wasn't the class for me. I eventually found my mentor; I tell the story in chapter 10. But it changed everything for me.

I ended up on a path that brought me to helping myself by helping others. And even as I'm writing this book, my journey is far from over. I feel every day is just the beginning—new lesson, new life, new adventure.

4

Spirits versus Ghosts

One of the most frequently asked questions I hear is: "What's the difference between a spirit and a ghost? Aren't they the same thing?" The simple answer is that there absolutely is a difference.

Spirits have crossed over to the other side (where and what that is I'll explain later), and ghosts are stuck—some believe on earth, others believe between this world and the other side. Having crossed over, spirits are able to come to us to visit, help, and guide us. "Crossed over to where," you may wonder? If you have ever read about spirits or spoken to someone who works in the spiritual world, they may talk about different dimensions or planes, i.e., "the sixth dimension," "the twelfth plane," and so on. I don't really get hung up on all that, but what I do know is that there are different levels on the other side. I consider these levels to be like grades based on how evolved the soul is: the bottom level is for darker souls, then going upward the souls become more evolved. The higher levels are for master teachers.

My clients often ask me: "Are my loved ones together? Did they meet up once they crossed over?" You should not fear that your loved ones are not together on the other side because souls that are connected find each other. It doesn't matter if one soul is more evolved than another; the souls that are more evolved just have more information about how the universe and the collective (what connects us all—the big picture of what is happening) works than souls that are not as evolved. My guides—spirits from past lives we have picked to help us in this life—as well as the spirits of loved ones who have come to visit explained to me that souls can and do interact with each other.

The soul evolves through experience and life's lessons. It is those hard times in life when we want to crumble and hide but instead we take a deep breath and keep moving, emerging out of the hard times stronger and wiser, that helps our souls grow. We learn some things when times are easy, but it's nothing like what we learn in the tough times. Think of difficult periods as checklists of things that must be done. Whenever we succeed in moving through a lesson, check it off. If we go through a hard time and do not learn the lesson, it will repeat again until we do get it—I've seen it happen in my life and in my clients' lives, in all kinds of scenarios. The key is to look at a situation and ask yourself "what did this teach me?" instead of wondering "why did this happen to me?"

Once I was speaking with a spirit who came with one of my clients. He was a very wise soul, very evolved. He informed me that once we cross over, we continue to learn and evolve by helping living humans move down their paths. At first my thought was, "You mean we don't get a break? I thought crossing over was peaceful and awesome!" He told me that it *is* amazing without the struggles, temptation, pain, and suffering, but our work is only beginning once we cross, not done. He said that it is extremely rewarding to guide a living human through a lesson to help his or her soul evolve. It can certainly be frustrating because humans don't always learn the first, second, or third time, but never giving up and working harder to learn can help not only the living human's soul but the spirit's as well. I always knew spirits were around us 24/7, but it really was comforting to know that they truly do have our backs and even though it feels like they don't, they do. Remember that everything happens for a reason; even if we have no idea why, we need to trust that everything is getting us to where we are supposed to be.

Our goal as souls is to graduate to the point of no return—literally. Imagine never having to return to learn lessons, only staying on the other side to guide and teach. Are you on your last incarnation? It would truly be amazing if you were, but most of us are not even close ... people

like the Dalai Lama are close, to give you an idea. Sometimes I meet people who tell me they're on their last human
life and that someone told them this. What really happened
is that they went to a medium or psychic who dropped the
"lucky you" line. It's awesome for you if it is true, but chances
are they are wrong. If you truly were on your last life, you'd be
a teacher and guide for us mere mortals. You would not be
coming to me for answers or to others—we'd be coming to you.
You'd be so evolved that you wouldn't need the help of a psychic or anyone else. Actually, I think you wouldn't need to get
answers, you'd understand how the universe works. You would
also be so evolved that you would rarely create karma. You'd be
above most human emotion and live in a place of acceptance
and knowing. Please don't freak out if you are readings this
and you believe or were told this is your last incarnation. If
this is something you feel strongly about and it helps you move
through life easier, I say grab on to that belief. (But I'll probably
see you in the next life.)

While we are on the topic of the other side, I get a lot
of questions about hell—is there a hell? I'm sure you've
heard all about that fire and brimstone in movies, books,
TV shows, and maybe growing up too. Guess what: we are
living in hell—yup, that's right, earth is hell. Here is where
evil does its thing. Think of all of life's temptation, struggle, suffering, desire, conflict, judgment, pain, and illness.
On the other side there is none of that; it is only peace and

knowing. Here on earth we need to learn to overcome hardship and evolve as a soul.

Spirits come to visit us often, whether just to stop by and see how we are doing or to guide us to make the right decision and move toward learning our life lessons. Spirits can and do visit multiple people, moving where they are needed.

Unlike spirits, ghosts are souls that have not crossed over yet. They live in a place or dimension that is between earth and the other side. I always feel like I need to defend ghosts because they often get a bad rap. I have a soft spot for most of them, even the frustrated and mean ones. Many times, ghosts are victims or in a state of struggle—they need our help. Furthermore, not all ghosts are evil or horrible—they can be scared, frustrated, or in desperate need of assistance. Some of them are nasty, but really, they are just humans who are stuck in the void. Are other really horrible, nasty entities out there? Absolutely, but they are not ghosts, so let's not lump them together.

Why or how does a soul get stuck and become a ghost? There are many reasons. Many people think it's because of tragic or sudden events, like a homicide or a traffic accident. This is certainly the case sometimes, but not always. Our soul knows when it is time to leave but our body does not, yet free will is always there.

There are two main beliefs I commonly encounter among spiritual world types when it comes to death. One is that we have many exit points in our lives; points where we can choose to stay in this life and move toward the next exit point. Basically we decide "nope, this isn't my time" and through our actions or lack of actions we miss an exit point. The other belief is that we truly only have one exit point and no matter what, that is when we are meant to die. If you have a near-death experience and do not die, it is because you were not meant to at that time and thus you were meant to go through that experience. There are many, many stories of people who were in a serious car accident and came out with only a scratch; often times they will say, "I guess it just wasn't my time to go yet." Which is the correct belief? Personally, I have seen the latter one play out time and time again; no matter what, things happen the way they are supposed to for both the person leaving this life and the people staying. I often tell my clients and students that a death teaches us many, many lessons. If we embrace those lessons, we can move forward. If we refuse and get stuck in grief, learning becomes much more difficult.

Souls that don't cross over right away (ghosts) can be souls that feel frightened to cross over due to certain events in their lives, e.g., limiting spiritual/religious beliefs or fears or the feeling of unfinished business with people still living.

The fear that keeps us here can be of many things, but a big one is a fear of punishment for misdeeds or mistakes in this lifetime. Most of this fear is rooted in religious beliefs; many humans believe that they will be judged once they cross over. The spirits have told me, however, that this is not true. Indeed, the question of judgment was one of the more important ones I had in the early years. Are there pearly gates? Is there an entrance to the other side with an ascended or master teacher or guardian angel standing there with a clipboard or a huge scroll announcing which people are going to heaven, hell, or purgatory? The answer was always the same, no! Although we have free will and make mistakes and generate karma, we will not be "punished" in the sense of being locked out of the other side.

As mentioned earlier before, the universe does most of its "punishment" on earth, not really in the traditional correctional or reprimanding sense. It is karma, the idea that what you put out shows what you will get back. Some believe karma comes back tenfold or even hundredfold, but the idea is the same: if you do something horrible, it will come back to you. Karma is in place to allow us to grow and evolve as souls. It is hurtful at times, but remember that it is meant to teach us. The universe is not going to punish you for making mistakes in this life by keeping you in limbo. If you generate a large amount of karma, you will deal with that in the next life. Likewise, if you didn't learn some lessons you were supposed to learn in this life, you will learn those in the next as well, possibly not evolving (learning) as a soul. Think of every life you live as an opportunity to move up a grade. You come into a new life with a mission to learn specific things to graduate to the next grade. If you do not learn those lessons, you won't graduate and will need to take those lessons again until you do. This is why we need to embrace our lessons (the hard times).

Some spirits explained to me that challenging lessons become tougher the more we do not learn, leaving us with no choice but to learn them. Sometimes clients' loved ones on the other side have informed me that the client in question has had many lives yet has not learn many lessons. The client may have lived a hundred lives but was still more or less a young soul. Having an old soul does not necessarily mean having a wise soul.

A number of spirits gave me this explanation: when we die, we cross over and then sit with our gatekeeper, the main guide we picked to help us in this life (all guides are explained in chapter 9), and go through our Akashic records. The Akashic records are the collection of information said to be held in the astral plane (let's keep it simple and call it the other side). Some call it our book of life, as it documents the soul's journey, including past lives, emotions, relationships, and karma. It is the book or place in which we design the next life. It tells us who we were and what lessons we learned or didn't learn. I always tell my clients it is like a debriefing. We cross over, get debriefed (it can take weeks or months), and then start helping living people by guiding them or giving them positive energy when they need it.

Many clients of mine worry that they themselves or others may become ghosts and be stuck in between forever. Chances are you will *not* become a ghost, but if you do, know that all souls can be crossed over. Even souls afraid of punishment or judgment may still see the light and cross over with the help of a medium or the soul of a loved one from the other side.

I have had a few opportunities to help souls cross over; while it can be done, it is not easy if the soul in question does not want to go. Many mediums find it to be an extremely rewarding experience. My most memorable was with a family member who died and felt they had unfinished business in life. This ghost stayed in my home for months. They would follow me to my meditation classes and on occasion attempted to talk to me through one of my associates. This ghost's energy was extremely disruptive (I have them to thank for the expense of a couple new televisions) because they wanted attention and a solution to a situation that was unfixable. Besides frying a few electrical appliances, their energy was so strong that they also would bring in a really negative vibe.

Every soul has unique energy or what I call an energy fingerprint. Whether you are living or dead, it is an energy that identifies you. Even if you can't see a spirit or ghost with your physical eyes, you can learn the difference between each spirit by getting to know their energy. You can usually tell by this energy fingerprint whether the spirit/ghost is female or male, happy or sad, positive or negative, and so on. I find that the longer it has been since a person crossed over, the more gentle and loving their energy becomes, but they will still have that energy fingerprint from the most current life they lived so we will know who they are. A personal example of this is my father. He was someone who loved and thrived off of chaos and disorder; if something was going wrong, he was in his glory and when all was running smoothly, he was miserable. After he passed away, he would come to visit me and his energy fingerprint was exactly like that. Almost twenty years later, when my mother was dying, it was my father who came to take her to the other side. I was surprised for many reasons, least of which because my parents had been divorced for a very long time. Although part of me knew my mother still loved my dad, I thought she would rather have one of her sisters come. When I spoke with my guides about this, they informed me that many souls are connected from the many lives they lived together. My parents had shared many, many lives together. My father's spirit visited me months before and his energy had changed—although it still had that fingerprint of loving chaos, it was much more loving. I would guess that his soul had evolved on the other side, but in order for me to know it was him, he allowed me to feel his old energy. I found it difficult at first because he was so different. His was an energy I could work with, provided I could forgive him for the things he did in my life, but could I actually forgive him? After a few weeks of him popping in and out, I realized that he had changed as a soul. This process was a huge lesson in my understanding of how a soul changes after crossing over and that even on the other side we grow and evolve.

I attempted to cross over the family member who was a ghost with unfinished business several times with no success. I tried everything I could think of: I called in the ghost's other family members who had crossed over, and the ghost would simply leave when they arrived; I attempted to smudge my house with sage, but the ghost would just come back a few days later; I tried different prayers, salt, reiki, calm reasoning, and arguing—the ghost would not budge, even when I told them that their presence was hindering any kind of healing that could take place once they were crossed. The spirit was not willing to understand that by not crossing over and staying to "fix" the unfinished business, it was just creating more unfinished business. After months of trying different things, I begged my guides and loved ones to bring in anyone who could help this situation.

Then one day I was going about my business vacuuming my bedroom, and the ghost was following me around telling me how to do things and how of course I did everything incorrectly. I turned to let the ghost have it when a shimmer caught my eye. I turned toward where I saw the bright multicolored shimmer and saw the spirit of a man I didn't know come walking out of the shimmer. He told me his name and turned smiling to greet the ghost. His energy was absolutely amazing; I immediately felt at peace. He was an average size man with graying hair, and as strange as this sounds, he had a glint in his eye. His energy was kind, gentle, and fun, and I could tell instantly that the ghost really liked this spirit. The man held his hand out to the ghost, the ghost walked toward him and took the gentleman's hand. The man leaned toward the ghost and spoke very softly into the ghost's ear—I couldn't hear what he said, which was annoying. He straightened and then turned away, holding the ghost's hand. They took a few steps together, the shimmer reappeared, they stepped into it, and then they were gone.

I was completely shocked. I stood in the room staring at the place where they had just exited. Who knew it was going to be so easy. The ghost just *left*! After months of struggling, I was left with a numb feeling. There was no major send-off… no epic fight or begging, they simply left and crossed over like it was nothing. Once the shock wore off, I picked up my phone and called my husband, Steve. I described the kind spirit and told him the name, and he knew exactly who it was. Apparently, the kind gentleman was exactly as I described in life, and it made a lot of sense to Steve, as the man was a favorite and well-liked person in the family. Well at this point, let's just say that I wasn't very pleased with my darling husband. After months and months of dealing with this ghost, Steve knew of this man all along but told me he just didn't think of him. I was relieved in the end to know that the spirit had finally crossed over and would be in a place of peace and love, no longer stuck.

Other souls can also be afraid to cross because they do not want to meet up with other souls. Just like us living people, some dead people have fears that are so strong they prevent them from crossing over. In one instance, I was at someone's bedside when they died. During the day I had seen a spirit couple standing in the one corner of the room and was informed that they were the woman's parents; they were there to welcome her soul to the other side when the time came. As the lady passed, I watched as her soul rose from her body. She seemed confused at first, but as she started to walk around the room looking at all the living people she was leaving behind, I could tell she was slowly understanding what was happening. She moved from living person to living person, standing in front of each of them saying her goodbyes, and every so often she would glance back at the couple. She was not going near them. I could sense the fear and knew that she would not go with them. I later found out that this woman did not have a good relationship with her father; she was afraid of him and angry with him for things that happened in their lives together. There was no way she was going to go with him anywhere. The woman's soul also appeared to have unfinished business, so she was on a mission to stay and clear some things up.

Unfinished business is tough because these souls are usually on a mission that can be good or nasty. The ghosts I have encountered that have unfinished business are extremely difficult to cross over, least of all because sometimes the "business" may not even exist anymore. The soul may be waiting for other family who actually passed on years ago and are already across; they may be attempting to fix something that cannot be corrected in this life or they feel their work is incomplete.

I came across an instance of unfinished business in a restaurant where my husband was the executive chef in an area of town that was older but growing. At the time, people were purchasing older buildings and renovating them. My husband complained to me that the restaurant was experiencing many unexplained disturbances, so I went to investigate and see what I could do—did it just need an energy cleansing or did it require a clearing of spirits? Upon arrival, I quickly realized that there were a large number of dead people in the building. I attempted to cleanse the property with very little success.

Most of the dead people in the restaurant were ghosts; a few spirits were visiting as well. Over a few months, the ghosts population and activity in the restaurant increased. The staff was even starting to experience physical ailments such as dizzy spells, upset stomachs, anxiety, and headaches caused by the number of ghosts. They were also experiencing a higher than normal amount of paranormal happenings that were really affecting their work. Stoves would turn off in the middle of service; some saw the knobs actually turn! Items would be moved and found in the strangest locations, and so on—the list of events and activities was absurd.

My husband begged me to do something, and soon after I met the ghostly woman who was causing it all. She was pacing behind the bar while I was walking around investigating. When I approached her, I realized that she was a ghost who seemed aggravated and on some sort of mission, but overall wasn't nasty. When I spoke with her, I found she was not very pleased. She was tiny and had white hair sticking out from underneath a bonnet-style hat. She was dressed very similar to what you'd see an Amish woman wearing. She told me she was a puritan and did not agree with what was happening on her land. She was unhappy with the alcohol being consumed and some of the other things happening. Apparently, she helps people settle when they come to the area, setting them up and helping them find their way. She was seeking and waiting for family but in the meantime was continuing her work. As the homes in the area were being renovated, many ghosts were in an upheaval. This ghostly woman invited them to her place so she could care and nurture them. She had set up a hostel for ghosts, more or less.

I told her the situation, broke the news to her that it was a different time than she was used to, and told her to stop inviting souls into this space. She was not pleased—actually, she refused to listen. Sometimes it can be very difficult to persuade ghosts because they are people … without physical bodies. They still have the same emotions and temperament, but also have the ability to disappear. So when I tried to talk to the woman, she'd just vanish! I told her I was going to help her across. She refused, saying she had to help; with all the souls that were showing up constantly, she strongly felt her work was not done.

I attempted to cleanse the restaurant using sage, incense, prayers, holy water, reiki—you name it. I went through all the normal practices for crossing the dead over, but this woman was not budging at all. On a positive note, I was able to cross over many other ghosts that were there, so the energy did adjust and the staff began to feel better. However, I could not get this woman to even think about going across. I called in the big guns and brought my mentor down with a few others. We attempted to cross her over together. After a few attempts, my mentor just laughed and said what I had already figured out: this ghost was not going anywhere, so the only thing that could be done was to live with it. In times when the energy became too strong because there were too many dead people, I'd cleanse it. The staff just had to learn to check and recheck the stoves and tell her to stop when items disappeared.

My husband moved on from this restaurant, so I'm not sure what the situation is today. I have a feeling the woman is still there, as I've heard stories from some friends who have gone to the restaurant recently. The staff is having issues with drinks getting toppled over or strangely falling off the bar. It sounds like she is still unhappy with the drinking.

The follow-up question to "Is there a difference between ghosts and spirits?" is "How do you know the difference?"

Spirits and ghosts feel completely different: Spirits are light and give you those nice chills that run through your body, almost like a nice breeze. Ghosts are dense; when you walk through their energy, it is like walking through water or really thick humid air. My thought is that ghosts feel that way because they are still grounded in this dimension, giving them more physicality. I also have found that because ghosts are more dense, you can pick up on whether the energy is positive or negative more quickly, keeping in mind that there is a difference between frustration and negativity. One of the most important things to know is that you do not have to be afraid of a ghost. If it does feel extremely negative, then yes, you need to remove it, but remember to stay calm and in control. The ghost is in your space, and you have dominion over that space.

Both ghosts and spirits use energy to manifest, whether to show themselves or move objects, and some are better at this than others. The most commonly used source of energy for dead people is emotion, followed by electricity. Remember my earlier example of *Monsters, Inc.*—fear is the easiest for them to use, so stay out of fear and stay in control.

Speaking of control, don't be afraid when ghosts and spirits seem to crowd you. They have a difficult time with personal space, tending to get very close. You might need to tell them constantly to back away. Not only is it freaky to have someone talking to you nose to nose, it can make your energy do strange things, depending on their energy.

If the spirit is hyperactive, your heart might start to beat fast; if they have strong energy, you may find you get dizzy. If you ask a spirit to back away, it should; ghosts may not at first, so be firm. Never feel bad about asking a spirit to leave your space, they will listen and leave, but they might return (loved ones especially). Remember that spirits have no desire to scare or hurt us: they love us so much and at times it causes them to come too close.

Removing a ghost that does not want to leave an area is extremely difficult but not impossible. It is a process and may take a while. The best way to remove a stubborn one is to take control and stay in charge. At the very least, if the ghost will not leave, it must live under your rules, not the other way around.

Spirits and ghosts are everywhere. I laugh when people ask me if they have spirit around them—I'd be more worried if you didn't! We are never ever alone, whether our company is one of our guides (always with us) or loved ones who have come to visit and help. It is very comforting to know we are being watched, guided, and loved constantly.

On a funny note before I end this chapter, I must talk about the fact that for some bizarre reason, bathrooms are extremely active areas. I have discussed this with many other spiritual types, and they all have different theories. The most common is that the ions in water are a conductor of energy that dead people can use to manifest. Any time you are around water, activity can be higher whether it is a bathroom, a waterfall, or a dam. Personally, I receive many messages while in the bath or shower and have to kick dead people out of my bathroom daily in order to get ready in the morning! Some are spirits I know, others are related in some way to the clients coming for a session that day. The number of experiences I have heard about from others relating to bathrooms is staggering, and in fact, some people receive their most important, powerful messages and life path clues while in the shower or bath. Next time you go in there, you might want to listen intently or at least take note of any thoughts that pop into your mind.

I have had so many different experiences with both spirits and ghosts. They drive me crazy but I love them. I work with spirits to help people and I'm driven to help ghosts. It drives me crazy when I watch these ghost investigation shows where they go to a location and provoke the spirits. Imagine having a horrible or tormented life that may have led you to do some bad things or you were a victim of a horrible act like murder and you are stuck because of fear. In walk these strange people from a different time who invade your space, start yelling and screaming carrying around strange machines, and then once they have tormented you all night they just walk away ... talk about frustration. I have only ever seen one of these ghost hunting type of shows where the people in it would actually attempt to cross the ghosts over. I know some ghosts will not go, but shouldn't we help them if we can?

I get asked often about my most memorable ghost experience. There have been many, but one of the most embarrassing was in a grocery store. It was a holiday and I was busy running errands. My final stop was to pick up groceries for the holiday dinner, and the store was packed and bustling with energy. Crowded stores are usually tough for me, but at the time I had no choice and needed to get this done. I pulled in my aura, focused on a tunnel of vision in front of me, and didn't allow my eyes to wander. I hurried through, picking up everything I needed. When I was finally in line waiting, I tried to focus on the Christmas carols that were playing over the store's speakers to relax my energy. I listened and hummed and watched the people in front of me with overflowing carts of holiday treats. Suddenly, the woman who was standing directly in front of me in line caught my eye. The first thing I noticed about her was that she appeared to be on edge. She also didn't have a shopping cart or groceries with her. She kept looking around as if she was waiting for someone. I assumed she must have jumped in the crazy long line to save a space while whoever was with her ran around the store to pick up the items they needed.

The person in front of this agitated woman put their groceries on the counter, which seemed to greatly increase this woman's fear. I had no choice but to watch her constantly look back and forth. I noticed that although it was winter, she was wearing only a sweatshirt and a pair of jeans. She was a tiny bit shorter than I am, with blonde hair that was up in a ponytail sticking out from the back of her pink Nike baseball hat. Her pink sweatshirt was nice, but she was really under dressed for the December weather in southern Ontario; the temperature that day was hovering around -10° C (14° F). The person in front of her finished paying, so it was the lady in pink's turn to pay for her items but the person the lady in pink was waiting for still hadn't arrived, or so I thought. I made eye contact with the cashier, rolling my eyes indicating my frustration with the lady in pink, sending a nonverbal message to the cashier like "give me a break, what's this lady thinking?" The cashier looked at me like she was confused and then just as she opened her mouth to say something, the lady in pink disappeared in front of my eyes! I was shocked. I was so focused on getting in and out that I didn't notice the difference in the lady's energy—she was a solid ghost.

When I think about it now, the encounter was actually pretty amazing—the woman in pink was as solid as a regular person to me but the cashier didn't see her. Her energy was very grounded to earth and so similar to a living human's energy that I didn't notice she wasn't living. I leapt forward in line making excuses of being off in la-la land and unloaded my cart as quickly as possible. I needed to get out of there and away from all the people who must have seen my display of craziness. I was so embarrassed. I was also not in a place in my life where I was okay with saying, "Yeah, so I see dead people, and a lady was standing in front of me just now and she just disappeared." I paid and left quickly. Once I had loaded all my groceries into my car and returned the cart, I sat in my car and laughed at myself and my crazy life. Then I had a sad thought—was the lady in pink stuck in that store? I decided to head back in and try to see her again. I walked around but did not see her. I have gone back a couple times since this experience to see if I'd run into her again but have never crossed her path again. I hope she has found peace and has crossed to the other side. I think she must have been attached to or following one of the other customers; when they left, so did the ghost.

As I said at the beginning of this chapter, I could speak about ghosts and spirits all day. But if you take away only one thing, it is to know there is a huge difference between the two.

5

The Usual Suspects

Most days, my house is like Grand Central Station. Some spirits come to speak to me about clients, others show up because they see the other spirits or because mediums are like beacons for the dead. I often think of it like mediums are patio lanterns and spirits and ghosts are moths attracted to our light. In addition to myself being a medium, both my children have my abilities and also attract spirits to them. So I guess you could say my house is like a lighthouse for dead people.

I try my best to ignore spirits I do not know directly and cleanse my house daily to make sure there are no negative energies around. Usually the first thing I do after my husband leaves for work and my kids are at school is light some incense, say a prayer of protection, and ask any spirits that are not connected to a client coming to please leave, informing the spirits that if they want to speak with me about a living person, they need to go out into the universe and through synchronicity bring their living person to me or someone similar to me to pass on their message. This is not an episode of *The Ghost Whisper*; I'm not going to track down spirits' or ghosts' living loved ones.

For readers who have similar abilities, your house is probably as busy as mine! With all the visitors I have on a daily basis, there are a few ghosts and spirits that stay in my home most days; I've taken to calling them "the usual suspects." Most people, whether they are mediums or not, have their own usual suspects, spirits that stay around a lot of the time. I have asked my guides why these spirits/ghosts hang around and found out that there are many reasons. Our loved ones appear to guide us, coming and leaving when needed, but some stick around and rarely leave. Why does this happen? Why are these souls with you rather than another family member? What I have learned is that there is usually karma with these souls (good and bad) as well as a very strong past life connection. It's most likely you and spirits/ghost of this nature have spent many lifetimes together.

I have a handful of usual suspects. My mother pops by to see me at least once a day and though she doesn't talk at all, her energy makes me sneeze (indeed, when she was alive she was known for her sneezing fits). I just say hello to her, she hangs out for a bit, and then goes. It's funny because when my mother was in the hospice dying, we had a discussion about talking to the dead. My cousin, my mother's sister's daughter, loves anything paranormal and had gone on a haunted house tour in Nova Scotia. A medium was there giving readings as part of the tour. When my cousin sat down and had her reading with this medium, her mother came through with many messages and wonderful, kind words. When I told my mother this, she told me not to expect her to speak to me when she crosses over; she didn't like that. She doesn't talk, being true to her word, but I think it's awesome that she at least shows up. I'm really lucky to know that she is around me and feel her energy, even though there are times I'd love to have a chat with her ... maybe one day.

There are currently two other ghosts mixed into the usual suspects who have been here since we moved in more than ten years ago. One is a very kind older gentleman who wanders my house. After a few discussions with him, I have determined that he is searching for his family. He says they lived in this area and he can't find them now. I have explained to him several times that he'd be better off crossing and finding them that way, but he refuses and says he can't cross until he finds them. He has frightened my son a couple of times by simply appearing in front of him. I know he is not trying to scare him and just wants to say hello, but my son is not okay with seeing him. I have had to very firmly set boundaries with the older man and insist that if he doesn't want to cross over, he must stay hidden in the basement and never attempt to show himself to any of my family. So far he has done what I asked, and every once in a while I will ask him if he is ready to cross to the other side. But he remains in my basement.

The other ghost is a young girl dressed in a white night-gown with long, wet dark hair. She is afraid of me as well as most adults who come into my home. She will dart across the room quickly to get away from adults, leaving a streak of white energy that even people who normally do not see Spirit will see. A few of my neighbors have commented to me about having strange activity happen in their homes, many stories about their children seeing a young girl. The neighbor directly beside me came over one morning to tell me that during the previous night, they were all asleep and she was woken up by the sensation of someone in her room. When she opened her eyes, she saw a young girl in a nightgown standing in her bedroom doorway. She assumed it was her daughter, so she told her to go back to bed and that she'd get up and tuck her in. When she got up and went into the daughter's room, the daughter was fast asleep. What freaked her out even more was that the daughter was not in a nightgown at all—she was in a t-shirt and pajama pants. I informed her that I was aware of the strange little girl and that she was harmless and to not worry. Up until a few years ago I was not able to get any infor-mation about this little girl due to the fact that I can't seem to get her to stay in the same room as me. Fortunately, a cli-ent of mine brought her son to speak with me regarding his struggle with his gifts, and while we were speaking, the little girl came out. This boy saw her and started to speak with her!

She told him her name was Allison and that she lived on the land, but when she alive, it was big fields, not houses. She informed him that she was abused and died running away from a man. She ran into a pond and drowned while the man simply stood on the shore and watched her die. In her ghost form, she is wary around adults because one abused her and others never helped her. She followed the young boy home and stayed with him for about a week only to return to my house. He attempted to get her to cross over to the other side but she was too afraid. Allison doesn't really affect anyone in my home; though my kids will see her on occasion and she dashes here and there, we more or less are used to her. One thing that's fun about her is that she will stand behind the door going into the basement, which is right by the kitchen table where I do most of my readings, and she will bang on the door as I proceed through the reading. Sometimes it's a fast knocking, other times it is a slow thump. Usually I try to ignore the knocks if the client doesn't notice, but sometimes it is so obvious that the client will say something, and I have to inform them that we have a ghostly audience that likes to participate at times. There seem to be some people she will bang on the door for and others she will hide from. She will always come out when I'm doing a session with children or teenagers.

My husband Steve's grandparents also visit often; although they are not here daily like the usual suspects, they show up enough that they are almost in that group. His grandfather doesn't speak to me but will unplug the phone from the wall to let us know he is around. When the kids were really young and he did this, I would have to tell him to please stop because if one of them was sick and the school called, I'd miss it. He kindly stopped during the hours they were at school, but once they were home I'd spend the evening plugging in the phone to only have it unplugged a few minutes later. Steve's grandmother is like a bull in a china shop. She stomps around the house and bangs so loudly that we can't ignore her. She usually pops in once or twice a month to give Steve and the kids some strength and energy to get things done in life. Her energy in death is just like it was in life, all about getting things done and being strong. It is a reminder that we can do anything and we shouldn't limit ourselves or our thinking.

On occasion, other family members and friends pop in to visit from the other side but they usually don't stick around. Along with my daily Mom visits and the two ghosts who live with us are two other spirits who spend most days here. The first gentleman is a spirit I call Mark. In life, Mark was a well-known athlete. He is connected to my husband indirectly in this lifetime but Mark has told me they were brothers in a past life. Mark came in one day while I was doing reiki on my husband, who was having a stressful time at work. I set up my table in our bedroom, making it comfy with pillows and blankets. I turned on the *om* tape I love to listen to when I do reiki, lowered the lighting, and lit a number of candles to create a beautiful, calm atmosphere.

Usually when I do reiki, my client's guides or loved ones will come in and help me with where I need to focus and adjust the energy.

My husband had just lain down and was getting comfortable when I picked up on a spirit in the room. It wasn't one I had felt before and I couldn't see them physically, so I ignored the presence and prepared to do the treatment. I had my hands on my husband's back, focusing on adjusting the built-up energy around his shoulders. I allowed the reiki energy to flow through me and into my husband when I looked up—standing in our bedroom was a man. The only reason I recognized him is because he wore a specific uniform for the sport he participated in as well as a few other trademark things he was known for. The fact that he was standing with his equipment from his sport also helped me put two and two together. As I stared at him standing next to my bed, trying to sort out why he was there, I realized I should first ask my husband if this athlete had died. Steve told me that the athlete had died a couple years earlier, of an overdose. Since that day this spirit has only left a handful of times but for the most part is here to help guide my husband. Mark also goes out with my husband and to work with him, only once in a while will he stay with me at home and sit in during my readings.

After a number of months, I was speaking with the spirit about my husband's nutrition, and the spirit informed me that he would get someone for me; he wasn't the person

I needed to speak with. A few minutes later, he returned with another gentleman who was dressed in the same uniform type so I knew he played the same sport. I did not recognize this other person though I could see him clearly. I described him to my husband. The man had a name in another language as well, so I was having a difficult time hearing it. We rushed to the computer and typed in athletes who played the sport who had died and looked at the photos. After looking for a few moments, there he was. I was shocked that we were able to find him so quickly. This other spirit is kind and gentle for the most part, much quieter than the other gentleman, but there are certain things he does that drive me crazy.

The second gentleman (we'll call him Will) came to help me with my husband's nutrition. My first full day with him was one of the strangest of my life. After my husband had left for work and my kids had gone to school, Will immediately started ordering me around. He told me what to do and how to do it. I felt like I was almost channeling or in a semi-trance state. Will told me about things I had in my pantry I didn't even know I had. Following his advice, I made homemade granola bars, energy balls with dates and nuts, barley salad, bean salads, roasted chickpeas, roasted peas—so many things I can't remember all of them. By the time my kids got home from school, there were dishes all over my kitchen.

Will comes grocery shopping with me and is the one spirit I have to be careful not to talk to out loud to when I'm out. He orders me up and down aisles and constantly tells me what to do, so I get frustrated with him. He is like an older brother, lovely but can be totally annoying.

Every morning, Will tells me what to make my husband for breakfast; he really—and I mean *really*—hates it when I cook an egg and break a yolk. He will start pacing and demand I cook a new one if the egg isn't perfect. Will says there are small pleasures in this world and a perfectly cooked egg is one of them so it needs to be perfect. I can tell you that I've perfected my egg cooking because of him. Will told me that in a previous life he worked with Escoffier, a master French chef from years past. As a result, he is quite passionate when it comes to cooking. Thank god I'm used to living with a chef and am familiar with their tendency to want perfection.

We have nicknamed Mark and Will "the boys," and they come with us most places but especially to the market or food shopping. The most amazing story of spirit manifesting in the physical I have is because of the boys. My husband, the kids, and I were driving to the market one day. Before leaving, my husband asked me if the boys were in the car. I told him they were: Mark was in the back trunk area and Will was sitting between the kids in the back seat. As we're driving, my daughter suddenly starts freaking out and brushing herself off. She said she thought there was a spider or a bug on her, then she found it and held it up—it was a piece of blonde hair about an inch long. My son started doing the same thing and also found a hair, same color and length. This happened about five times going from kid to kid. My husband spoke up and said, "I didn't have anyone in the car," thinking I would freak out that he had a blonde in his car. I laughed so hard, I was crying. Once I calmed down, I looked at him and said, "Who do we know with that color hair and length?" At first he couldn't think but then it clicked and he couldn't believe it. It was Will. Just before my kids noticed the hair, my husband asked if Will was with us, so Will decided to prove to us that he was there. I have heard of angels doing this with feathers. They say that if you are somewhere and a feather appears out of nowhere, it is a sign that an angel is around you.

Mark and Will have totally become part of our family, though Will seems to be more connected to me. He says he is connected to me, Mark, and my husband all from the same past life, but I've never asked what precisely we all did in that past life. I'm curious but more focused on the now. Mark helps me decorate, telling me where to hang pictures and changes I need to make. I have to say he has really good taste, so I never doubt what he tells me to do. Will is all about health, fitness, and food. Will believes in a simple whole way of eating. It is about moderation and going back to our roots. Hungry? Grab an apple. Going on a bike ride? Grab an apple.

I re-read this chapter and realize how bizarre my life may seem, but for me it's normal. I have a wonderful support system. The boys are always there for me. I have to laugh because if my husband and I have an argument Mark always gets protective and will not answer any of my husband's questions for a few days. He holds more of a grudge than I do. Will rarely leaves me and makes me feel loved and protected, even if he does boss me around at times.

If I have an issue whether it is cooking or with work, I turn to them and ask them. If they do not know the answer they will either go and find the answer or direct me to find the answer.

The only time Mark will not aid me is if the energy is dark. He says he had too many experiences in the past with the dark to mess with them now or anytime. He is also crazy superstitious and is constantly telling us to adjust things that may bring bad fortune. Don't EVER put a pair of shoes on a table, especially new ones ... the man freaks.

I love the boys and I am so blessed to have them in my life. Life is never boring with them around. I also realize that sometimes Spirit comes just to visit and reconnect with us. Other times they are here to guide us and help us, by synchronicity or by giving us the energy or a positive boost we need to move forward in life. Sometimes they need to create an upheaval in our lives to make us move forward. With this knowledge, I've been able to look at things differently and realize it is true everything happens for a reason, even if we don't see clearly why in the moment, it is leading us to where we need to be and we are never alone. Spirit is always around helping us.

6

Negative Entities

This is an important chapter for many reasons, the least of which is because many of us who do sense and see spirits but have not honed our gifts are terrified of negative spirits or ghosts. It's tempting to lump them all into one category—"scary"—but it is necessary to know what really is out there and how to handle it. Once you understand these kinds of spirits, it is possible to release fear and be in a position to take control. Much of the information that circulates about spirits is fear-based, and the popularity of ghost hunting and paranormal shows on TV only help the more sensationalized information flow. This chapter is about the darker side of things, for clarification and to allow you to get rid of any fear you have regarding negative energies or entities.

As much as I'd love to say there are only good spirits and ghost out there, it isn't true. I'd be lying if I said that if you work in the light for the good of all, you will never encounter one. There are many different types of negative spirits, ghosts, and entities. Some have negative energy that can affect our moods and energy, others are nasty and—I'm not going to sugar coat it—they're horrible... but still not to be feared.

As stated in a previous chapter, there are levels on the other side: the bottom is for dark souls that have not grown and are miserable and nasty, but they are still spirits, not ghosts. The next level up are what people call the tricksters—these are souls that aren't completely dark but love to mess with us. As far as I have learned, these are the two levels on the darker side of the spirit world. Completely separate are the mean, angry, scary ghosts. I always think of ghosts as living people without physical bodies. If a person was mean and angry in life, chances are they will be the same as a ghost. Remember also that frustration is not the same as cruelty and anger.

The main nasty category most people lump all ghosts and spirits into is the D-word, demons. Yes, demons are horrible, and yes, they are evil, and *yes*, they exist! I consider demons as the opposite of angels: beings just like angels that never lived as humans.

In all my years of having my gifts and working with them professionally, I have only had a few run-ins with any darker entities. When I asked my guides why, they stressed that a lot of it has to do with the fact that I'm strong- rather than weak-minded. I teach this same idea to my students.

We must stay in control, in charge of our minds, bodies, homes, and workplaces. It's our domain and no one else's!

My first experience with dark spirits happened when I was about fifteen or sixteen. It was an experience that I will never forget but want to at the same time. If I was faced with it now, knowing how to deal with these kind of energies, it would be a different situation, but back then I was clueless and a complete victim to this dead person lurking around.

A bunch of family was living in Tewksbury, a suburb of Boston, where we'd go every summer to visit them. If we were not in Tewksbury for summer vacation, we were in Cape Breton, Nova Scotia, which was ghost-filled and exhausting. I thought Tewksbury would be much better until I had the worst summer of my life. We were staying with my aunt and uncle, and when we arrived at the house, I immediately noticed the energy in the house was dark and spooky, which was strange as it was normally a house full of light and laughter despite the suffering that was going on with my aunt's illness (at the time, she was struggling with cancer).

I thought the energy was strange but really had no clue how I could figure out why the energy was off nor did I want to—I was happy in my state of "ignorant" bliss. Unfortunately, my aunt's condition had worsened; she was a walking skeleton but still had a smile on her face and was up for a laugh. I found her attitude inspiring. She may have been terrified and crying behind closed doors but in front of me she was strong and in control.

The first night in the house, I could not fall asleep. I remember being painfully tired, as we had gotten up really early to fly from Toronto to Boston. However, there was no way I was going to close my eyes and drift off to dream land this night—I could sense a dark energy moving through the halls of the house. Every once in a while I'd hear a quiet scraping sound on the hallway walls that was so soft at times that I'd convince myself that I was imagining it. The negative energy would decrease and increase as the spirit or ghost would move away or come closer to my room. A couple of times, I attempted to close my eyes to fall asleep but could not keep them closed…I knew the energy was getting closer. I did not want to see what it was but at the same time couldn't look away. If it was going to come at me, I needed to be aware. I cowered in my bed with my covers pulled up to my eyes. My eyes stung with exhaustion, and it hurt to keep them open. My body was aching with the desire for sleep. Moonlight was streaming in through the blinds of the bedroom window and leaving slashes of light on the floor and walls, making the whole scene even spookier. I kept my eyes glued to the doorway as I could feel the negative energy building. The spirit/ghost was getting closer.

Suddenly, a dark shadow crept into the doorway. It was as if my body forgot how to breathe, my lungs refused to function. I held my breath so long that my head started to spin; if I continued to hold it any longer, I was going to pass out. I slowly let tiny wisps of air escape through my mouth, because there was no way I'd release a large breath and let this shadow that filled the doorframe know I was aware. I'm sure it could feel my fear but my goal was stealth, pretending I was calm and cool (what a laugh). Looking at the figure, I realized it was definitely male, extremely large, and not very nice. I could not see any features clearly; the best way I can explain his appearance is that he was darker than the darkness. On a side note, I want to clearly state here that many people talk about shadow figures in a negative way. What I have learned about shadow figures makes me feel I need to defend them. Not all shadow figures are dark, evil, and mean. Many are spirits who can only manifest as shadows, or seeing dark shades could be how your gifts allow you to see them. For this reason, it is *really* important to feel the energy of a shadow figure should you encounter one. It might just be your late grandmother, not a sinister entity!

The amount of negative energy coming off this shadow was unbearable—I can only relate it to what it must feel like to be stalked by a lion or tiger. I felt like I was his prey and any wrong move on my part would allow him to move in for the kill. I know now that could never happen, but at the time I was terrified. It occurred to me that not only was I feeling this dead person's presence, I was also seeing him. My ability to blind myself to the dead people and not see them did not seem to work in this case. My ignorant bliss, which I worked so hard at having, had taken wings and was out the window. That was it—I was *not* sleeping, no way, no how. The dark figure would stand at my door stalking me. Although I'm sure it was only minutes, it felt like hours before he would then slowly creep away, moving further down the hall only to return a while later. He did this all night. I'd just pray for the sun to come up, as if the sun would magically make the dead person disappear (I knew it wouldn't but my belief in safety in numbers gave me a sense of security). Once the sun was up, so was everyone else.

After a painful night, I found my uncle awake and in the kitchen making coffee. I rushed out and stuck to him like glue for the rest of the morning. There was no way I was going to be alone in the house, ever. I forced my uncle to play a game of cards with me. He was a good sport and although I'm sure he had a million things to do, he sat down and entertained me knowing that once my mom and aunt were up, he'd be free to do his own thing. That morning I realized the summer was going to be very long; I had four more weeks of sleepless, terrifying nights ahead of me. I wish I knew then what I know now, but all I could do then was quickly adapt to survive. My aunt and uncle had a big pool, so I'd go out and "sunbathe" (sleep) poolside. I was becoming one big freckle. I'd glance at my image in the mirror and wonder how it could be possible to have so many, I was running out of space they were joining together and becoming spots. I was transforming into a Dalmatian. Rainy days were spent the same way as sunny days. I'd go into the backyard under the large gazebo and "read" with my eyes shut.

The rest of my vacation nights at that house went exactly like the first: cowering in my bed, sheets up to my eyes, staring at my doorway, sensing the energy moving around the house, and praying for the sun to come up. Interestingly, the entity never came into my room, never venturing farther than my doorframe. To this day, I'm not sure why. I think about it sometimes and wish I could go back to find out. I wonder if he isn't connected to nearby Salem, the location of one of the largest and most documented witch trials in the US; the city is only a half hour away from Tewksbury. Was that entity a dead person from the infamous witch trials of 1692–93 or someone who hunted or prosecuted the alleged witches? Since I had the ability to see dead people, did this spirit think I too was a witch? If I was alive and living in Salem in 1692, I would have been classed as a witch for the abilities I possess. It would make sense that this entity felt that way about me as a result. I believe now that this energy/entity was a ghost; the feeling was too dense and thick, completely different from any other dead person back home. Ghosts and spirits feel completely different. This energy was not light and tingly like the spirits I was used to—it was dense and heavy like a ghost.

When our stay was over it was the best day ever—I'm not a great flier but I couldn't get on that plane fast enough back to Toronto and back to my state of ignoring the dead people.

I did go back a year later to Tewksbury to help my aunt and uncle move back to their hometown in Cape Breton, Nova Scotia. My aunt had decided she wanted to pass away and be laid to rest where she was born and raised. I was reluctant to go back to Massachusetts, but I loved my aunt and wanted to help where I could. When my mother and I walked up the steps to my aunt's front door, I remember bracing myself for what I'd find once I entered the foyer but the house was quiet. There was no sign of the dark, negative ghost; it must have moved on. I wasn't about to question the situation, but I was tense the whole week waiting for him to return.

It was explained to me years ago that some ghosts love to prey on human energy and use bodies. All ghosts and spirits use our energy and energy around them to manifest, whether to show themselves to us or move things around. Trust me when I say it takes a *lot* of energy for them to be able to do this. Many ghosts want to experience the human body again to move about in the physical world. When they do this, it is similar to being possessed but more like being a ghost's puppet. The only way a ghost can take charge like this is if the person they want to use is weak of mind or invites the ghost to take over their body, as they cannot enter the body of anyone who refuses to allow them. One way to weaken your mind is using alcohol and/or drugs. Many spiritual workers do not drink for many different reasons, so for my beginner students just learning to hone and control their abilities, I always advise them to watch their intake of alcohol or drugs. These substances drain your defenses and unwillingly open your third eye. This vulnerability is why many negative ghosts gravitate toward bars—people who indulge in too much alcohol are easy targets.

When it comes to anything negative—negative ghosts in particular—I always teach that they should never be provoked. We need to remember that these ghosts are (were) humans who for some reason are angry and negative. To put it another way, would you walk into a situation with a really angry and unhinged person and start yelling at them and poking at them? If you had to go into that kind of situation, you would most likely be strong and firm but would not anger the person even more. If they did somehow feel provoked, you'd expect that person to attack.

I understand that many investigators provoke ghosts hoping to get a response, but I wonder why anyone would do that to the ghost and themselves. In many cases, the ghost will follow you home and create chaos in your personal environment or worse, it could follow you around, attaching itself to you and using its negative energy to affect your energy. The ghost would make you feel the way it feels—angry and aggressive.

Whenever I do an investigation and a clearing, I teach protection techniques to the property owner. One of my most memorable experiences came after getting a call from a very upset woman whose family was being terrorized by a ghost. Another medium and I went to the location and found the woman outside her house sitting with neighbors. We did an interview with her and her neighbor who had both experienced the activity. So many things had happened to this poor family, but the most common was a man who appeared most nights to her children with a rope around his neck. This man would say mean things and try to make the children do mean things. After our discussion, we decided to take a tour around the house. Instantly I sensed the man: he was not hiding, he was moving quickly through the house. There was no question he was a ghost, but his mental state was more confused than malevolent. He went from being loving and wanting to be around people one minute to angry, frustrated, and confused the next. We picked up his name and the information about him: he was mentally challenged and had been accused of inappropriate relations with children. His family owned the land this woman's house now sat on, and at the time of his death his family owned a large farm. He was angry with the people of his time for being mean to him but was also very scared of people. He ended up taking his own life in the barn by hanging himself. Additionally, the other medium and I also sensed another, darker energy around this home. We were pretty sure it was the d-word, but it hid and would not come around us. I knew it was trying to take advantage of the family's fear and weakness. The medium and I cleansed the house and put up protections, asking the homeowner to assist us. We gave her strict instruction on how to take control of her property and not to be afraid.

A few days later, I heard from the woman again, and she was very excited. Her neighbor had gone down to city hall records and did research on the information we picked up. Sure enough, she found information regarding the family and the gentleman. She was also able to locate a photo of him, which they showed to the children. The children confirmed it was the same man. Finding all this information gave the woman the power to take complete control. Although he was not going to leave the property, she was able to make the ghost stop scaring the children and disturbing their home. She also informed me that the day after we left, she was outside talking with the neighbor. At the time she had her baby monitor on and heard something growling through it. She stomped back into the house fearlessly and told whatever was messing with them to get out of their house and leave them alone. The growl stopped immediately! This woman was now empowered to deal with any spirits or ghosts she would encounter in the future, which will likely happen as her youngest son is gifted as a medium.

Another important thing to remember to do after an encounter with anything negative—spirit/ghost or even a living person—is to cleanse yourself, making sure the negative energy doesn't follow or attach to you or leave any negative energy in your aura. There are several different ways to cleanse, but the first thing you must always do is to brush off your aura, removing the energy surrounding you by brushing off your body with downward strokes. Think of it like brushing off lint or snow from your clothes. With both hands, start at your head making your way down toward your feet with quick brush strokes, shedding any energy that may be stuck to you. Once you have more time and are in a better place to do so, you can use reiki on yourself, smudge with sage, or have a cleansing bath. I recommend to most of my clients and students who are gifted to cleanse themselves daily, if not monthly. I personally do daily protection and monthly cleansing baths, and if I come across something or someone extremely negative, I will do it more frequently.

Here are instructions for my favorite spiritual cleansing bath:

Fill the bathtub with warm water. Add 1 cup (or more depending on how you feel) table salt or sea salt, half a box of baking soda, 3 slices of lemon, and 7 drops of one of these: sandalwood oil, frankincense oil, bluestone, or another essential oil. (Perfume is okay in a pinch.) Wash your whole body, rub the lemon on your body, and make sure you also dunk your head under the water. Do not rinse off. When you get out, air dry or pat yourself very gently with a towel. If you only have a shower, get into the shower after mixing the ingredients in a bowl or bucket and clean yourself with this water. Do not rinse yourself off with the shower water. Get out once you are finished and air dry or pat yourself off very gently with a towel.

Dark souls and the tricksters are an interesting group. The same rules apply when dealing with these souls as dealing with ghosts: strong mind, stay in control. Dark souls are easier to pick up than tricksters because you can feel their negativity immediately. Their energy feels different from that of a ghost, lighter and more like a spirit (since they are on the other side), but they are aggressive and angry. I have come across a few dark souls doing sessions with clients. One thing I find with them is that they will listen and you can completely stand up to them and remove them. They do like to hang around living people to whom they are connected, bringing that aggressive, angry energy around them. Because they are spirits and on the other side, however, they function similar to a more evolved soul—they are around to teach us lessons but teach them through negative emotions, usually bringing up past hurts and insecurities, temptations and fears.

In the grand scheme of things, even dark souls are trying to help us grow and evolve, despite their nature. The question becomes: do you get pulled down the dark path or do you go toward the light? Dark spirits work by pulling us toward the dark with the actual goal of turning us away from them, pushing us toward the light. My mentor and I discussed this many times: when we are moving forward in our life, making things happen and we are feeling good, it seems like all of a sudden things start going wrong. She explained that as we get close to certain achievements (that is, learning a life lesson), the dark rises up to test us. Do we keep moving forward or do we fold and retreat? Do we look at something not working out as a failure or an opportunity? Although these souls in particular work more in the dark, it is still to move us forward. I know it's hard to wrap your head around it, but the dark and the light work with each other for the ultimate good.

Tricksters—now these souls are tricky. (Yes, I just said that.) Although tricksters play with us, again I truly believe they can ultimately teach us, but they kick it up a notch from the darker souls, which tend to be a bit more negative and miserable. I think of dark souls like dealing with a grumpy uncle who's known for being angry and grumpy and everyone deals with him knowing that. Tricksters can pretend to be someone else, sweet as pie, giving you good information, but when you trust them, they will lead you astray.

I had a few experiences with tricksters when I first started honing my abilities. They would pretend to be someone's loved one on the other side, give me just enough information that was correct, and then they would start saying really strange things to confuse me and the person I was reading. It made me feel like I couldn't pick up the correct information, so I thought I wasn't good at doing readings. It also gave the person I was reading mixed messages, confusing them and sometimes hurting them emotionally. Tricksters attempt to place doubt in our minds, and I honestly believe they do it to help us learn and grow. I learned so much from my interactions with them and have heard others with the same stories. Once I learned to only work with the highest and best, they never tried to deceive me. When we work with spirits, we should always ask to work with our highest and best. Keep in mind, however, that we are all at different levels of soul evolution; my highest and best may be different from yours. My guides taught me that spirits will only share what we can handle or absorb.

Working with tricksters ultimately taught me how to really feel spirit energy and ask the right questions. It also taught me to work closer with my gatekeeper (a guide). Now when I do a reading for anyone, myself included, I make sure that my gatekeeper screens them, only allowing them to speak to me if they are the correct soul for my client and come in the spirit of the highest good and best for all of us.

What spirits tell me now is completely different from what they told me when I was first honing my gifts. I think of it as being in grade one and learning age-appropriate math; if the teacher started teaching you algebra, you'd be lost and wouldn't understand anything. The same applies to information we receive from Spirit. As we learn and grow, they share more and more. Therefore, our highest and best evolves and changes. The spirit of your deceased grandmother will still come to visit and give you support, but if she doesn't have the information you require, chances are another spirit will come forward who has the highest and best information for you.

One question I get quite often from my students regarding the two lower darker spirit types is what to do if a client's highest and best is one of these types? In all of my years working, I have never seen that happen. I've helped clients with unfinished business with a darker soul where that soul appears for the client to work on letting go, but there is always a more evolved spirit there to help guide the healing/reading. Also, if the client's highest and best was one of these darker spirits, their energy would be dark as well and you would pick up on it immediately.

If you decide to continue a reading for someone whose highest and best is a darker type spirit (or if the person is a friend), you must protect yourself from their energy and the spirits around them (see chapter 7 for more about protection). Most times, these types of people do not gravitate to light workers, so chances are you will not run into anyone like this. These kinds of people usually turn more toward darker arts and practices.

This chapter would not be complete without discussing the nasty of the nasty, the d-word, demons. They are smart, tricky, and will use whatever tricks they have to in order to make you weak so they can take advantage of you, similar to a trickster spirit but for a completely different purpose. They will be friendly and kind, giving you correct information at first so you trust them, but many times they work through temptation as well as intimidation, after which they will take over. Whereas a trickster spirit will mess you up and confuse you, bringing in doubt, a demon's ultimate goal is to destroy your life and others; it wants control. They will turn you away from everyone and everything good, making all of your thoughts negative and dark. Some demons will attempt to possess people and take complete control, but if you are strong-minded and protect yourself often, you will be safe and these awful beings will stay away. They do not want to waste their time with someone they will never be able to manipulate.

In the years I have worked professionally and even before I honed my abilities, I have only come across a few of these nasty things. My first experience happened in my own home, when my children were very young and I had been honing my abilities for a few years. The energy in my home suddenly shifted; one day it was light and happy, the next it was dense, and I could sense something was not quite right. It felt like someone was lurking around, watching, and ready to pounce. It's a very paranoid feeling. Even the house itself felt instantly creepy. The feeling is hard to explain; even with the ghosts I'd experienced that scared me, nothing felt like this—it was creepy and evil … just nasty!

Over the next few days, everyone became tense. I was fighting with my children and husband, we were all losing our tempers, and no one was sleeping. There was also an increase in paranormal activity in the house, which normally has a lot going on most days but this was different. There was a lot of scraping on the walls and chairs moving in the kitchen. On a few occasions, doors would open and close on their own. Again, I had experienced some of this kind of activity with spirits and ghosts, so during this increased activity I tried numerous times to figure out who it was to no avail. The energy felt sneaky, stuck to corners, and low to the ground, almost like it was crawling instead of walking around.

After a few days of the strange activity, things started to take a different turn. After we would all get into bed for the night, the pipes in our house would start to moan and rattle. The house itself is not old and we use the taps often. As I was taught to remove the physical presence, I knew I would have to suck it up and go into the bathroom. I got out of bed and approached our bedroom door, and I could see and feel a presence that was like nothing I had encountered before. It moved like a dark mist or water. I first saw it on the floor outside of my bedroom leading to the kids' bathroom and their bedrooms. It slowly moved along the floor and made its way up the wall to the ceiling and into a corner. As I stepped out into the hallway, the energy felt like walking through mud. I say that ghosts are dense, similar to walking through humid air or water, but this was thick like nothing else I had encountered. I took a deep breath, attempting to clear all the fear from my body. I repeated over and over in my head that I was in charge, I was walking with the light, and that I was protected, nothing could affect me. Back then, I was doing a lot of faking it to make it; it took a huge effort on my part not to freak out. At least I had learned in dealing with ghosts and spirits to never show fear and never give them that energy.

During this walk from my bedroom, which felt like hours but was only seconds, the pipes were still moaning and groaning. As I entered the bathroom, the noise increased and it sounded like a person moaning rather than the pipes. I turned on the taps to see if that would stop it but it didn't. In fact, the sound seemed to be coming up from the drain rather than from the taps. I stood in the bathroom and demanded that whoever was doing this had to stop and leave my property. At this point, the fear completely left me and I was getting angry, but then I realized that this was not the right thing to do because the demon wanted to use an extreme emotion of mine to gain power; whether it was extreme anger or fear, I was not in control. So I took a deep breath and stayed calm, firm, and in charge. It continued for about another ten minutes, and the whole time I stood repeating over and over for it to leave and that it was not welcome. I called in anyone from the spirit world who could assist me to remove this being from my home and keep it out. Suddenly the energy lifted and the moaning stopped.

I instructed my kids to call in their grandmother if they felt scared, that she would protect them always and keep anything scary away. It was important that we were all on the same page, and I wanted to get them to take ownership of their space and not be afraid.

The strange sounds continued for a few weeks, same thing every night. I started to do a lot of research on how to remove something so nasty; at that point I knew all I wanted to do was remove it but not investigate who or what it was. This is when I learned the benefits of salt. I read about how many different religions and spiritual practices use salt to repel or remove ghosts and worse. Salt is said to have a purifying quality that evil and negative cannot and will not cross, or if they are around salt, it will absorb the negativity. After two weeks of the moaning and feeling the bad energy, I put a plan in place: I did my usual routine and once I felt the energy shift and the nasty presence leave, I put salt in every room in my home. I then cleansed the house and put a salt perimeter around my home as well as on every door and window frame. The evil presence was *not* getting back in any time soon. The moaning stopped after that night and I never felt the energy again. I think this success was due to the combination of my family staying mentally strong and unafraid and the salt and protection I performed.

The incident with the evil energy taught me that it is essential to have protection. These days I salt my house regularly and cleanse it daily with incense. If you want to do the same with salt in your home to absorb negative energy, you need to dispose of it after a few days or up to a week. Make sure you don't get rid of it on your property, as well. I usually dispose of it on our compost days and put it into the compost to be cleansed by the earth. The salt I disperse outside my house that has absorbed negativity will usually get washed away by the rain or snow. If it hasn't been cleared away after a week or two, I will wash it off and then salt the area again. The easiest way for me to remember when to replace all the salt is by the moons—when the moon is full, I change out the salt.

My experiences have taught me that there really is nothing for us to fear, whether it's a negative ghost, a darker spirit, or even demons. Nothing can hurt or affect us if we stand strong and do not let it. Experiences with negative forces have also helped me to connect more to my abilities, trusting and believing in them strongly. Following are some prayers that can also offer strength and reassurance.

Prayers of Protection

Dear Universe,

Remove all negative energies and entities around us. Send them to their proper planes and fill them with love.

Close the aura of each of us against those and any other negative energies, and in their place, put the highest and most powerful vibrations of light, love, and peace. Now cleanse, clear, fill, and encircle each of us in the white light of healing and protection.

Thank you.

The light of the universe surrounds me (us).
The love of the universe enfolds me (us).
The power of the universe protects me (us).
The presence of the universe watches over me (us).
Wherever we are, the universe power is!
We rest in the universe as the universe rests in space.
And we accept only that which is the highest and best.

Holy art thou, power of the universe!
Holy art thou, whom nature hath not formed.
Holy art thou, the vast and the mighty one.
Lord of the light and of the darkness.

7

Energy

I pull my car into the farthest corner of the parking lot, away from other vehicles and the hustle and bustle of crazed shoppers. Putting my car into park, I glance around, close my eyes, and take several deep breaths. I go through my routine carefully to prepare myself for the energetic tidal wave I'm about to dive into. I use these techniques daily and have taught many of my clients and students to use them as well. The first thing I do is pull my aura in by visualizing it closing around me with every inhalation, like sucking all the air out of a balloon. My aura envelopes me like a scuba suit or a costume that completely disguises me and makes me invisible to the spirits and energy around me. I'll be able to get in and out with as few issues as possible. Once I feel my "disguise" is in place, I say my prayers of protection and relax all the muscles in my body, starting from my toes and slowly moving up to my head. Next, I tunnel my vision so that I only see what is right in front of me. I turn off the car and step out into the big, dangerous, and scary world of the wholesale store. With every step I take closer to the door, I repeat my prayers of protection and repeat to myself my mission, just like a Navy Seal. My mission: get in, recover the goods I need, and get out. I have my tools (my membership card) at the ready as I walk up to enter the doors. There can be no delay; this mission must go seamlessly. Eyes forward, head held high to never show weakness, I grab a shopping cart, swing it toward the doors, and enter. The crazed energy hits me as soon as the doors clamp together behind me. I've committed now, I must continue. I'm feeling confident until I brush past a few customers, picking up their negativity and stress. I swerve to the right, entering one of the towering aisles, and my energy shifts again. I'm feeling like a scuba diver submerged under the water with my oxygen quickly running out but I'm drowning in the energy coming off all of the items towering over my head. I look down at my shopping list and use it to refocus myself, playing my mission out in my head. I take a few more deep breaths, shake off as much of the energy as I can, and keep moving.

I move swiftly through the store picking up all the items I need. I know I need to finish up because I can feel my aura slipping and slowly unraveling around me. I make it to the checkout in record time. I pay for my items and head out. Mission complete. Now I need a nap.

For some of us, going to a big-box store or mall is difficult because these places are like energy bombs: the items tower over our heads, basically drowning us in energy, to say nothing of the energy coming off of the customers, staff, and any dead people that may be around. It sounds intimidating but don't freak out. It is still possible to visit these places, but you just have to know your limits and use the techniques listed in this chapter (especially numbers four through nine) to deal with those situations. Once you learn how to deal with being in public, you'll feel much better. The more balanced you are, the easier it is to deal with it.

Energy affects us all, yet no one stops to think about how. I believe energy should be the first thing to get a grip on or at least understand before attempting to master your "gifts" or even just understand yourself better and why certain things affect you the way they do. As the world advances with technology, there is more and more energy around. It is not a great thing for people like myself; I often want to move to the outback of Australia to escape all the energy around but that wouldn't be productive ... and, honestly, I'd miss all my clients and Netflix.

Until you understand energy and the effects it has on you, you will never be able to balance yourself enough to get a grip on your gifts, whether you are a psychic, medium, empath, or even a regular person who is sensitive to energy.

Energy is all around us, and everything is made up of energy. People, items, and Spirit are all energy. For some, our internal energy meter is higher than others, meaning we are more affected by energy. Everything has a vibration it throws out in order for us to recognize it. To put it simply, let's say everything from people to items to spirits are songs, and each have their own song. Some are classical, some are country, some are calm, some are rock, and some are even thrash metal. Imagine yourself as a person who is able to hear all those songs at full volume. Most people might hear tiny little whispers, some pick up nothing (there are days when I wish I was one of those people), and then there are those who have speakers or headphones on turned up to 11. (That's a *Spinal Tap* reference. For those out there who have no clue what I'm talking about, it basically means it's turned up louder than the dial allows it to be turned up.) Most mediums and empaths feel energy *way* above 11, and it can throw us off balance.

Mediums or "sensitives" are always more sensitive to energy. I've never met one who wasn't. If you look into the world of famous mediums, you'll find it easily: Theresa Caputo, "the Long Island medium," suffered anxiety; Carmel Joy Baird of "My Mom's a Medium" also suffered from anxiety; I myself have suffered it, and the list goes on. Some do not suffer as badly as others, but others really do. It all boils down to energy. Mediums are more sensitive to human energy and clutter, and Spirit makes it even crazier. I'm not saying that everyone who has anxiety is a medium, but I do believe people with anxiety may be more sensitive to energy they absorb into themselves which then affects how they function as a human. In my practice, I am constantly coming in contact with people struggling with managing their relationship to energy. It's among the most important if not number one thing to master.

Although it may seem straightforward, controlling incoming energy is a difficult thing to do. Because it can't be seen and only felt, sometimes we only sense it when it is pushing so hard on us that we finally connect the dots and realize what is happening. Once you become completely aware, however, it will be much easier to adjust and deal with the energy. Following are some techniques and examples to deal with the one thing that affects us all, whether we are highly sensitive or only slightly aware.

Although energy affects us all, empaths are affected by energy the most—whether the energy is from a person, place, or thing. Empaths have many traits, but basically an empath is someone who feels other peoples' emotions, ailments, and energy. An empath's life is unconsciously influenced by others' desires, wishes, thoughts, and moods. Classic signs of an empath are being overwhelmed in public places, a knowing that goes beyond intuition, feeling others' emotions and taking them on as your own, and picking up and developing the ailments of others. Empaths always look out for the underdog, as their sense for justice is extremely strong. In fact, empaths are a beacon for others to off-load their problem upon. An empath's moods will change depending on others' moods, and world events can be extremely upsetting.

What empaths need to learn is balance, to be themselves while protecting themselves. They need to learn how to not take on energy that is not theirs. They also need to learn to be neutral in their lives, learning what is their energy and what isn't. Understanding how energy affects the body can help with this greatly.

Different types of energy can affect us in different ways, so we need to know how to protect ourselves from the effects. Empaths in particular need to become aware of the shifts in their feelings, and what is (and isn't) theirs. People come to empaths and pour all their issues onto them. The empath absorbs and carries these issues and the people leave feeling energized and happy. The empath is left in need of a nap as well as now taking on the other person's emotions or ailments.

Some people take empaths' energy without knowing it, thinking only that their awesome friend gives them wonderful advice and leaves them feeling so much better and lighter after venting to them. They are not aware they just dumped their issues into the empath's lap and now the empath has to struggle with the emotions, worry, and despair. These are the people the empath needs to learn to balance; we can advise and be that awesome friend, but we need to not share our energy and should never take on others' issues.

People who know they are taking empaths' energy are called energy vampires. Yes, vampires do exist, but it's not blood they suck…it's actually the other life force in us—our energy. These people are horrible—they purposely go around sucking energy from anyone they can just to make themselves feel better. Empaths are easy targets to these people so if you are one, you must learn to protect yourself from these parasites.

Another issue for empaths is always being pulled into other peoples' drama. They get in trouble at times because of it, and the solution again here is to stay neutral in dramatic situations. Empaths need to learn to listen and *not* help. In a fight of six people, getting involved to solve the issue will only leave the empath feeling hurt and wounded.

Following are a few tips for empaths to protect themselves.

- Don't over-help. Let people walk their own paths and make their own mistakes.

- Learn to say no or at least "not right now, maybe later." You must follow your own timetable.

- Never carry anyone's issues. Listen, give a few words of support, and put the responsibility back on the person to fix it. Get in the habit of saying "What are you going to do about that?" instead of giving advice, unless asked.

- Say the prayer of protections daily. If you know you are about to talk with someone who is going to drain your energy, say the prayers again.

- Visualize your aura coated in a force field of white light. Surround yourself with white light, encasing yourself in love and protection.

- Suck in your aura close to you, making it a cloak of invisibility. This will keep your energy within your body as well as hide you.

- Call in Archangel Michael to protect you and to remove any negativity.

- Protect your chakras, especially your solar plexus. Hold your hands over it or fold your arms in front of it.

- Once you leave an area or a person, always brush off your aura. This will remove any energy that may be stuck.

- De-clutter your home and space. The more items around an empath, the more difficult it is for them to think properly. (This is covered in the next section.)

With these changes, your life as an empath will improve noticeably. It is a constant battle, but it does get easier. Empaths are born, not made, so the trait must be managed.

There are other things empaths can do to make life easier, but what I've outlined here is a place to start; sometimes small changes make the biggest dent.

When teaching students and clients, I usually start with the topic of clutter. For people who are affected by energy and especially empaths, the more stuff that's around, the harder it is to function. I like to show how energy affects us, as it is a tangible thing and has immediate results.

When you are working or at home and have a ton of stuff around, do you feel more anxious? Is it hard to concentrate, or do you feel a sense of being unable to focus, especially on more than one task? What about an overwhelming sense of not knowing where or how to start (which by the way leads to hyper-focusing and avoidance)? The hard part is that some of us have fooled ourselves into thinking that clutter doesn't bug us. Trust me when I say that it does; if we think it doesn't, we have only succeeded in functioning within and being used to clutter for so long that we know no difference. Try de-cluttering, organizing, and minimizing your possessions, and see how you feel. I guarantee it will shock you how much better you will feel; you will think more clearly, get more accomplished, and most importantly have more energy for yourself.

These days, I search for things to purge when we have bulk garbage days (large items). Purging is one of the best feelings for someone who is sensitive. It always makes me think of that old saying—cleanliness is next to godliness. It isn't true in the way we think as kids; the universe will not strike us down if we are messy. When we live in a clean area, we are clearer of mind and we can receive easier. We can hear messages or feel gut instincts and actually be able to enhance our lives by listening. A clean environment allows energy to flow and move without getting stuck and pulled; it brings balance.

My husband will read this chapter and laugh: what often happens to me is because of my own fears and my struggle with energy, I will start to hyper-focus over time, putting all my energy into one thing, be it clients, writing, avoiding, or something else. The daily clutter that comes into the house from kids and new purchases must be dealt with, so then I have to readjust and bring balance back into my life by not allowing the energy to make me hyper-focus. It is a struggle, though I laugh because I can hear exactly what one client's guide would say to that; he'd look at me very seriously and say, "It's not a struggle, it is simply a choice," which is easy for him to say because he's on the other side. I have to admit he is right, like Yoda when he said, "Do or do not, there is no try." I am not going to lie or sugar coat it, it is difficult at times, but we can all do it. When we are in balance, things flow better in our lives and we stop blocking things from coming to us. I always look at balance like a recipe, and in order for us to be the best us, we need a bit of everything on our card. We each have different ingredients that make us who we are, but we all need a bit of this and a dash of that to be balanced and whole. For me to be balanced, I need a bit of clients, writing, teaching, exercise, and creativity to make me whole. When I follow my recipe card, the results are amazing.

Once we admit to ourselves that we are probably affected by energy, we can start by de-cluttering or organizing the areas we work in or where we spend most of our time to see how we feel. De-cluttering and purging also creates a void that the universe will always fill, though not necessarily with more stuff; it will provide things we need like a job, people of like mind, or money.

The next step with understanding energy is to start to pay attention to how people's energy affects you. The best way I can explain this is that we all have our own unique energy fingerprint. If a friend of yours and I were to stand behind you, it would be possible for you to feel the difference between us (our energies) once you know to be aware of energy. The same is true with Spirit—if you cannot see a spirit but can feel them, you can get to know the spirits around you by their energy (e.g., masculine, feminine, young, old, and so on). You can recognize your spirit guides using the same practice (see chapter 9). A fun exercise to recognize people's energy is have one person stand behind you in a group of people and see if you can recognize who it is. Repeat this a few times. Even if you can't figure out who is standing behind you, see if you can detect the type of energy, i.e., masculine, feminine, and so on.

The downside to feeling or being affected by human energy is that when you go into a location with a lot of human energy, it may be overwhelming. You can quickly become tired, anxious, and/or your emotions may jump around. Imagine you are attending a wedding. You go into the reception hall and see that two hundred people are there. The average person feels the energy of those two hundred people, whereas myself and others like me feel all the dead people around as well. If the average person has two dead people with them (most have more), the population of that reception goes from two hundred to six hundred people, a *lot* of energy in one place! Furthermore, remember that I related different energies to music; imagine all those different types of songs playing at the same time and try to have a conversation. Malls and amusement parks are tough for the same reason, so stick to the techniques to make it easier. Personally, I have my limits and there are times where no matter what techniques I do I just cannot handle much. Maybe you know your limits already too.

Not too long ago, my family and I went into a big-box store to get my daughter new glasses. We were at the front of the store and I was doing fine when suddenly my son's energy sky-rocketed—he was picking up on some high energy as well. I told my husband to take him somewhere else. After buying the glasses, my daughter and I went to find my husband and son, and every step we took farther into the store caused my energy to up. By the time we left (really only really about ten or fifteen minutes), I was buzzing; my temper was flaring and I was having a hard time focusing. It was like a pot on a stove was on medium boil but then the heat (energy) was cranked way up and the pot started to boil over. For people who are able to feel energy easily, online shopping is a blessing.

You may find you have to use a combination of the techniques listed in this chapter or just one depending on how energy affects you and the situation. The one that works the best for me and many of my clients is sucking in or shrinking our auras. I found this technique very helpful when my mother was in hospice passing away from cancer. I'd enter the hospice and by the time I was finished visiting, I would only just make it to my car when I'd feel violently sick to my stomach. I'd have to sit in my car and do a quick meditation just to be able to drive the half hour home. I attempted every technique I knew but none worked. My mentor suggested I use reiki energy or earth's energy, so I attempted to pull energy from the earth so my energy would not be affected, but it did not work. I finally had a "duh" moment and asked my guides what to do. They told me I needed to almost disappear so the people in the hospice would not pull my energy—you can't use what you can't see—and the only way to do that would be to suck my aura in (for lack of a better word) or put on a disguise so I would be invisible. It worked, and now I use it whenever I'm going to be somewhere with a lot of human energy. I can only hold it for a period of time, but I can actually go where I wouldn't be able in the past without being affected physically somehow.

The next type of energy I'd like to cover is residual energy. This is the energy in an area, location, or item. Have you ever been in a friend's house for a dinner party and noticed that something is off, even though all seems well and happy? You can feel that there must have been a fight before you arrived. You are able to feel this because the home is full of the energy from the fight. In fact, residual energy is the cause for many hauntings. Many haunted houses are not full of ghosts or spirits but actually the residual energy left in the location due to a stressful or a repeated situation. Some paranormal investigation shows talk about "an intelligent response," which refers to an actual spirit or ghost responding. Moaning, humming, or whispers may be residual energy from things that happened before but are not necessarily a haunting. Have you ever sat in an intersection waiting to turn left and suddenly picture yourself getting in an accident, like someone coming through the intersection and T-boning you? This is not a premonition or you being paranoid—it is most likely you feeling a residual energy from an accident that happened in that location, and it can happen while driving down a street or the highway as well.

Though I'm sure I have always felt residual energy in my life, I was not aware of it until I started to understand energy. My first clear memory of residual energy is when I was in Scotland with my husband to visit his family and tour around. We went to Loch Ness, an experience I'll never ever forget. We woke early in the morning and I could already feel my body buzzing with anticipation. We had been in Scotland for a few days and I was slowly adjusting to the spirits and ghosts that were around. It's a whole different ball game in Scotland than in Canada. The house we were staying in was probably older than Canada as a country, and the experience was amazing but taxing at the same time. I have to say I was a bit disappointed that the day was sunny and beautiful. Apparently, we were visiting during some kind of weird heat wave (I have never seen more sunburned people in my life). I held out hope that once we arrived at the loch that the notorious Scottish weather would turn to its normal foggy and spooky.

My stomach was doing flips, I was so excited. As we came closer to the loch, the roads seemed to narrow a bit and the landscape became more closed in—the mountains that were in the distance slowly crept closer, as did the tree line. The road started to wind, and as we turned one bend I could see the loch through the trees and small cottages dotting the shore and hillsides. Then I saw it—Urquhart Castle, the famous castle ruins you see in all the photos of Loch Ness. My heart leapt into my throat, it was hard to swallow. I couldn't believe I was here! We toured around the village for a bit and I attempted to stay focused on the shops and the other sights, but my heart and mind were impatient to visit Urquhart Castle.

Eventually we made our way there, and as soon as I set foot on the land surrounding the castle, I started to pick up on movement and activity. It was really busy, and I could feel the energy of people from a time gone past rushing here and there, but at the same time it was comforting and I truly felt like I was home. Once I entered the castle itself, I became enveloped in the past energy. I could see people walking around in kilts and gowns. I could see servants and animals. I could hear voices, though not clearly. I ventured up into one of the towers and on my way down, the most incredible experience happened. I felt a tugging and was having issues moving down the tight stairwell. I looked down and saw that I was in a huge gown with a corset, and my dress was getting caught on the walls. There was a servant behind me pushing and pulling to free me. Eventually I made it down the stairs but I was having a hard time breathing because it was so overwhelming. I honestly didn't know if I wanted to run screaming from the castle or stay there forever. This happened at a time when I had no clue what to do with my abilities or how to use them. It is a memory of experiencing residual energy that I'll never forget, and I have yet to feel it as strongly since. I'm not sure if this is because there is a past life mixed in with it as well, but it was incredibly strong. The fact that the sun was beating down on us did not matter at the time; it had changed from a place of mystery to a place of comfort and love.

Residual energy is a fun thing to play with, so see what you can pick up in a location not necessarily with your eyes. It's also the reason why we must cleanse our homes and workplace regularly. If you are selling your home, I recommend cleansing your house daily until it sells, as you want your home to be welcoming and pull people in with warm and calm energy. Likewise, if you purchase a home, cleanse the house before moving in any belongings.

······················ **8** ·····················

Meditation

There are many forms of meditation. You do not need to sit in a certain position chanting certain mantras wearing certain clothing to meditate. Some meditation comes when we are doing something creative. To dead people, creativity is anything that makes our heart sing—for some it is making art but for others it is hiking, bike riding, or baking. We get so involved in creativity that we open up and let go of all the day's stresses and limitations—and *this* allows us to connect to the energy and the universe around us, allowing us to receive messages and relax. As I'm writing this book, adult coloring books are quite popular. It is said that coloring is as good as meditating or at least has the same calming benefits. I think that once people realize the importance of having peaceful moments, it may lead them to practice meditation. People meditate for many different reasons: becoming closer to the universe or pure silence; relaxation;

or connecting to Spirit, guides, or to their intuition, allowing them to receive messages.

Personally, I used to have difficulties with meditation. I didn't get it—I understood in theory why a person would meditate, but I didn't connect the dots to its real importance. Many of my students and others with whom I've spoken think the same way, but the truth is that if you stick with meditation, you will eventually most likely find it essential.

My first attempt to mediate in my mentor's class was extremely uncomfortable, to put it mildly. Like everything in life, however, I realize now that I had to struggle so I could teach others who struggle with it how to work through and overcome those struggles. My mentor held her class at another student's house in January, and the weather was typical for Toronto at that time of year: cold, snowy, and windy. I had a distinct feeling as I walked up to the house that this night would set me on a journey that would change my life completely. At the time, I was hoping it was going to be a life without seeing or hearing spirits, but once this class was over I knew that I was fooling myself if I thought I'd ever be able to stop it. As I approached the steps to the patio, the door swung open and I was greeted by one of the ladies. She ushered me into the house, quickly made some introductions, and then pulled me into the living room where a circle of chairs surrounded a coffee table that was covered in crystals and other strange items. My mentor greeted me. I had never met her face to face until this moment. She was welcoming and we had an instant connection. She led me to a seat beside her. She instructed everyone to get comfortable, to make sure our feet were flat on the floor and that nothing was crossing. She explained to me that the form of meditation she would be guiding us through was called developmental meditation. It was about learning to connect to Spirit and receiving messages while also receiving the benefits of relaxation from traditional meditation.

Once everyone was comfortable, my mentor signaled for the lights to be turned off, plunging us all into deep darkness. My first thought was WTF. As I've said in previous chapters, I do not do well in complete darkness or at least I didn't back then. I thought about how I was in a room with a bunch of strangers and had no idea what we were about to do. My mentor started us on our guided meditation journey, but I thought I'd landed in a nightmare. This was a horror movie, witches' night out, and a séance all rolled up into one. I worried that instead of making the dead people's voices silent, I would somehow make them louder after this.

I tried my best to calm myself and embrace the dark around me. I started following my mentor's instructions and found the breathing techniques quite helpful. It was fascinating just how tense my body was as we made our way through our body relaxing each muscle, starting with our toes. (Who knew how much tension we held in our butts!) She moved on to helping us to clear and balance our chakras, or energy sources in the body. After the chakra clearing and connecting us all with a white light, she talked us through the meditation. At this point, I started to get freaked out and extremely twitchy. I started to fuss and fidget in my seat. The more I tried to ignore an itch or ache, the stronger it got. And as soon as I started to get into the meditation, the dead people wanted to have a chat, not one or two of them, more like fifty. It was hopeless. I sat for the remaining class with my eyes and mouth shut, and when class finished I felt like I had run a marathon; it was not relaxing or helpful.

My mentor pulled me aside afterward and talked me into continuing. It took me a while to work with different techniques that helped me to actually get benefits out of meditation. I started with crossing my ankles and hands, which kept me closed off a tiny bit, so I was not as opened as everyone else was in the class. I was able to relax, focus, and let go. The next step was to take control of the situation when spirits came in—I would greet them and ask them to please allow me to meditate; if they really needed to talk to me, I would set up an appointment with them later during the week to sit down and connect to them. It sounds funny, making appointments with Spirit, but it changed many things for me—I was now working with rather than fighting to ignore them. After taking the few minutes at the start of every meditation to do that, I was then free to actually practice receiving messages for other people using different techniques my mentor was teaching. The experience was life changing, and though I may still hear them, I don't have to listen and could now have full two-way conversations with Spirit and be okay with it.

Now after many years of practicing meditation, I realize that while I may not have mastered it the way a yogi or a monk has, I am able to quiet my mind and the outside world. I can allow myself to let go and simply be for a brief moment every day. Silencing the spirits may take a few moments, but the more I practice meditation, the quicker this process becomes. Meditation really is vital in our high stress, fast-paced world; I didn't realize quite how important it is until I stopped meditating for a period of time. Without it, my life was completely out of balance.

Meditation is important for everyone, and as said earlier it can be found in many forms. Some need to practice the traditional meditation, while others find it in creativity. Creativity is different for all of us—relaxing and doing number puzzles may bring an accountant to a place of letting go of that outside world, stresses, and energies; for others it is painting, photography, writing, bike riding, motorcycles, or cooking. Whatever it may be, it must be something that takes you to a place where there is nothing but you and the creative. You should be able to let go of daily stresses and energy as well as build your energy and fill back up, giving you the strength, mental clarity, knowledge, and energy to tackle the next task or day. If sitting and meditating is too difficult and you can't let go, you need to add a creative

activity to your life to do the same thing—it is key to balance and finding your power.

Meditation brings me balance; it is the moment where
I can refill and re-energize myself, similar to plugging in a
cell phone to recharge. I can't function without meditating
daily, even if it is a quick ten or fifteen minutes to rebalance
my energy.

My advice for anyone new to meditation is to start with
a guided meditation. It is easier to let go and listen to the
journey the person is taking you on than attempting to do it
yourself. Like many parts of spiritual work, the key is to simply let go—no pressure, no stress. If you can't get through
the whole meditation the first time without fidgeting and
being uncomfortable, that is just fine; keep at it. I found that
if I was having one of those fidgety moments, I'd pick up an
item and try to connect to it with my eyes closed. Whether
it is a ring or a stone/crystal, hold it, feel the energy and
texture—is it warm or cold? Focusing on an item can help
you let go of the outside world and allow you to relax while
physically focusing on the item. The next time you meditate, hold the item but do not focus on it unless you find
yourself being distracted and unable to follow the guided
meditation. You will find you will be able to slowly focus on
the meditation rather than the item and eventually will not
need it at all. It is also extremely important to find a guided
meditation that works with your vibration; if the person's
voice cuts through you no matter how many techniques you

try or how popular that person is, it will never work. You must find a meditation led by someone whose voice calms and relaxes you.

Once you have become familiar with guided meditation, you can start meditating on your own. At this point, you will be able to meditate anywhere at any time. When I was ready, I started by listening to music or the *om*; now I can meditate in a noisy room or a quiet room. The other thing you will notice as you advance is you will become less distracted by the outside world once you are in the meditation. When I first started, I was easily distracted. If the phone rang, I'd nearly jump out of my skin. Now very little can distract me or pull me out of my meditation until I'm ready to come out.

I've mentioned how meditation is important for balance, but it can also be a tool to aid people who have sleep issues. If you wake in the middle of the night and have difficulty falling asleep again, you can use some of the basic meditation techniques to slip easily back into sleep. Very rarely will you need to go through the whole meditation process to fall asleep again. Relax your body by starting at your feet. Work through each muscle group and then clear and balance your chakras to remove any stress and blocks.

Meditation techniques are wonderful for people with anxiety. I think they are must-learn skills if you are struggling with anxiety, as the act of having the control and focus to relax each muscle in the body, as well as the ability to clear and calm your mind does wonders. I use mediation exercises in situations where I'm extremely anxious, such as flying. I'm not a great flier but love travel, so when I feel my body becoming a stiff board of tension as the plane screams down the runway, I start the process of meditation. I usually close my eyes (sometimes I keep them open) and start focusing on each muscle, starting with my toes. I will stay focused on each section until it completely relaxes, moving upward through my body. Once I'm finished, I'm completely calm and relaxed. If I feel myself starting to tense up again, I take a few deep breaths and picture all that tension leaving my body. My muscles and mind relax, and I feel myself sinking into my chair ... and the anxiety is gone!

When most people think of meditation, they think of Transcendental Meditation (TM), another practice of calming the mind and body. I teach what I refer to as developmental meditation and it is usually used in spiritual circles/groups. Although many of the techniques for TM relaxing and balancing are the same, developmental meditation also focuses on developing psychic gifts.

Developmental Meditation

Developmental meditation helps us work toward spiritual growth. It helps us develop our spirit/soul self or communicate with the higher spirit world, angels, spirit guides, Master Teachers, highly evolved souls, spirits, and so on. If we want to discover the abilities God/the universe gave us and how to use them, its methods and exercises are invaluable. Everyone is here for a different reason and learning experience, so why we are here will depend on the abilities we have. Everyone develops differently, so it is important to never compare your development with another's. We must have faith and trust in what we are receiving from the higher spirit world. Truth is very important, which is why we pray and always ask for our best and highest good.

Along with development comes responsibility. When you receive a message for someone, always ask if you may share. Never force a message on someone else, sometimes people do not want to receive and it is always their choice. If the message seems private or sensitive, pull the person aside once the meditation circle is closed and ask them then if they would welcome it. Give the message *exactly* as you get it. It is possible that the person rejects the message after you give it because they do not want to accept its contents. That is not your responsibility—yours is only giving the message. Sometimes you'll receive a message and do not know who it is for. Give it out anyway and see if someone claims it as theirs. Many messages come as a collection of symbols. There are universal symbols and symbols that have meaning only for you or the person. This will come with development. You can say how you feel about the message, e.g., whether it feels good, sad, happy, negative, and so on.

Students and clients often ask me what one technique or tool I could never live without, and my answer is always the same: meditation. It truly balances and heals the body, mind, and soul. Although I'm known for loving the divination methods I use, meditation is essential, and I'd never give it up. It can be done anywhere and anytime for no cost or expectation. I dare you to try it; give it a chance and keep at it, and I guarantee it will become as important to you as it is to me.

9

Guides

When I first started meditating and attempting to walk down the path to learn more about my "gifts," I was constantly hearing about spirit guides, gatekeepers, or simply "guides." The term confused me greatly. Everyone seemed to beam with pride over the relationship they had with their spirit guide, even to the point where having certain spirit guides seemed to earn them bragging rights. I was also confused as to the difference between a guide and the spirit of a loved one coming to help.

The topic of guides is sensitive but extremely important. There is a persistent miscommunication that gatekeepers or spirit guides (all are explained below) are people from this life here to guide us, like a grandparent or parent. This is not the case, and I do not want to shatter anyone's hopes and dreams that their family on the other side is not with them guiding them—they are and they do, but in a different way.

Our guides are only here to help and guide us, but our loved ones are here to help and guide most of the souls they were linked to in this lifetime. Going further, think of it like this: we have an inner band of guides and an outer band of guides.

The inner band are souls from our past lives we picked to be our guides in this life; they are not our loved ones from this life. These guides are here just for you, and I refer to them as an entourage. They never leave us; they work for us and assist us in completing what we came to this life to do. These are the seven inner band guides.

Gatekeeper

Your gatekeeper is your right-hand person, your personal assistant; they allow your lessons in or stop things—you just need to ask. This person is the one whom you should really learn to connect with. Even if you never see them (such as in meditation), it is important to feel their energy. The gatekeeper is the person in charge of keeping your Akashic records. They have your to-do list, and it is their mission to get you to check each item (life lesson) off your list.

When I really started working on my gifts, it was my gatekeeper with whom I worked most closely. Even though I'm not afraid of dead people, I still have my limits with my gift and am not really a fan of dead people talking directly into my ear. I can handle it in my head (third eye), or seeing an item move across the table, or walking into the kitchen and seeing that a man is sitting at my table, but physical talk in my ear is downright creepy! So when I started honing my abilities, I asked my gatekeeper to keep dead people in check—no voices in the ear, no gore, and no surprise visits. It worked and shifted so I was comfortable learning how to deal with my gifts. Before I asked my gatekeeper for help, my abilities were out of hand, very random. My gatekeeper took away the surprise spirit visits until I could handle them and slowly brought Spirit around, first when I was only meditating, then as orbs, then the orbs started to form an outline, and then full on spirit … and by the time this happened, I was able to deal with it.

One question I am asked quite often is: "What is my gatekeeper's name?" Many people are intensely curious about this, but it isn't all that important—chances are they've been around many lifetimes and were known by many names, and they couldn't care less what you call them. What's more important is that you feel them around you and know their energy so you can work with them. The best way I know of to get to know your gatekeeper and inner band guides' energy is through meditation. Before you start meditating, ask them to come forward and see if you feel a difference in their presence. You can do this for each guide to learn their energies.

Guardian Angel

We all have one, and some people have a couple. Angels are protectors and teachers, connected to the heavens (the universe), and the earth. Though these beings have never been human and are beings of the universe, they are here to help us spiritually and also in any other way we may need them.

Although angels are here for everyone, our guardian angel is directly linked to us. They are here to help us evolve as souls. Angels will take a physical form when necessary in order to guide or help us. We have all heard of those stories about a random person coming out of the blue at a horrible accident. They rescue or calm victims to only disappear afterward.

I'm awed by angels; though I have worked a bit with them directly, the only time I have ever seen my guardian angel was in meditation. I have never seen any form (e.g., no wings or body), only an extremely bright blue-white light. The energy coming off of the light is unbelievable, full of love and acceptance and strength and empowerment. It is the manifestation of knowledge that we are all worthy and capable to do anything we want to do. There is also a knowing that we are all one and all connected to each other.

Joy Guide

This guide comes around you to bring joy into your life and remind you that you need to enjoy life and relax. They also bring in high energy when you need it. Many times, they show up in dreams or meditation as little children. I've only seen mine a few times in meditation, in the form of a teen-age girl dressed in a cheerleading outfit, pompoms flying—not my style at all. I'm more of a casual, martial art loving person so cheering is not something that works for me. The few times I've seen her, it did remind me that I needed to relax and bring more joy into my life.

The joy guide helps us stop focusing on unimportant things and instead look at things with awe and gratitude, like a child might. They help us remember that joy is all around us.

When I am in a place of struggle to be positive and see the good, I will meditate and ask my joy guide to come forward with a message. She never fails me, and I always finish my meditation and time spent in her energy feeling grateful. Our joy guide's perspective is incredible, and it is based on the idea that there is no bad in the universe, only good. I hope you are able to connect to your joy guide... it can change your life.

Guide of Wisdom

This guide is a spirit who grounds you to the earth. For some it takes the form of a Native American Indian or aboriginal person but it doesn't have to, although most people who have seen their wisdom guide report seeing them in those forms. They are a spirit of a person who lived and was connected to the earth. They help you stay grounded to the earth. They are very spiritual spirits but they also bring the earth energy with their energy. They often have messages and lots of wisdom.

Some people use the term "Indian guide" as well. Having worked with mine, I think "guide of wisdom" is more fitting—you will find when you start to get to know your guide of wisdom that the energy is so calming and down-to-earth. They are extremely deep; with only a few words, they may change your perspective of a situation.

I find the guide of wisdom to be very Yoda-like. Although all guides have a deep knowing, this guide makes you really think about situations, the earth, and our connection to it and each other.

Many clients and students of mine see their guide of wisdom as an animal, thus this guide is also known as an animal totem. My guide of wisdom often shows up in meditation with an eagle. Other times, when I'm meditating with another guide, or relaxing or get messages, this eagle will be flying around in the meditation or be standing off to the side. It is a reminder to me that I must look at all perspectives and remember I'm just as connected to the earth as I am to the spiritual realms. These guides are wonderful for grounding and balance.

The Doctor or Healing Guide

This guide helps us with our healing work. They bring messages when you have an illness or when you get a message about someone else who is ill. Many people who have strong medical intuition have a very strong connection to their doctor/healing guide. Although an outer band reiki guide usually steps in when doing reiki, I find that my doctor guide or the client's doctor guide steps in to help when doing a reiki treatment on a client.

In meditation, your doctor/healing guide will help you in adjusting your energy as well as work on aiding any ailments you may have.

The Chemist Guide

This guide is here to adjust your etheric body (aura) to work with spirit energies. When you do spiritual work or connect to the universe, you have one foot in the physical world and one in the spirit world. The chemist guide also helps to keep you balanced, adjusting your body so you can receive messages and work with Spirit easier. I have always had a funny visual in my head of the chemist guide—to me they are like the captain of the ship. The gatekeeper may be the one leading the team, but the chemist is the captain of the vessel, adjusting energy here and there to ground you or allow you to let go.

Over the years I've noticed that most mediums have a tic of some sort: some click their fingernails, others bite their nails, some twirl their hair, and my nose runs or my eye twitches. When there is a high volume of spirits around me or I'm about to sit down and do a session with a client, my nose will start to run. I have to explain this to the clients so they understand I do not have a cold or allergies. Once the reading is finished, my nose will be fine. After speaking with my guides, I found out that this was my chemist guide's doing—he was adjusting my body to allow clear communication with spirit.

If you are having difficulty with connecting to Spirit, this is the guide you need to work with through meditation. Have your guide come forward and work with them closely to open up your chakras and adjust your energy so you'll be able to hear and see more clearly.

Psychologist Guide

This guide helps you with counseling yourself and others. Empaths and sensitives are strongly connected to their psychologist guides, which is why in part people are attracted to us and feel they can unload their issues on us. Our psychologist guide shines strongly though us, like a neon light sign above our heads that says "Help Here!" with a huge arrow pointing down at us.

These guides give us the right words and a knowing that aids us in helping others. They will also help counsel ourselves, giving us the information we need to see a complicated situation with more clarity. In meditation with your psychologist guide, you will be able to see all perspectives of a situation.

Although I've been doing this work and meditating for many years, I've had little one-on-one contact with my doctor, chemist, and psychologist guides; they tend to work through my gatekeeper. When I'm doing very specific work such as healing or life coaching and come across an issue I'm having difficulty connecting to, I will call them forward to work directly with them.

Below are some questions you can use when you are trying to get to know your guides. Just focus on your different guides, and as you meet them you can take notes if you want. Remember that this may take a while; your guides may slowly reveal their true identity the more comfortable you get with their energy. Again, the best way to do this is through meditation but you can and should try sitting quietly, calling one forward. See if you feel the difference in the energy around you or if you pick up their energy.

When you come out of meditation, see if you can answer any of the questions below. It may take you a while before you can answer even one of them, but write any small or large pieces of information you can remember to help you recognize their vibration when they are around you.

What do I know about my gatekeeper guide? Do I see/sense/hear my gatekeeper's vibration? Do I see/sense/hear what my gatekeeper looks like? Do I see/sense/hear what my gatekeeper is wearing? Do I see/sense/hear a name for my gatekeeper guide? Do I see/sense/hear a color or smell with my gatekeeper guide?

What do I know about my guardian angel guide? Do I see/sense/hear my guardian angel guide's vibration? Do I see/sense/hear what my guardian angel guide looks like? Do I see/sense/hear what my guardian angel guide is wearing? Do I see/sense/hear a name for my guardian angel guide? Do I see/sense/hear a color or smell with my guardian angel guide?

What do I know about my joy guide? Do I see/sense/ hear my joy guide's vibration? Do I see/sense/hear what my joy guide looks like? Do I see/sense/hear what my joy guide is wearing? Do I see/sense/hear a name for my joy guide? Do I see/sense/hear a color or smell with my joy guide?

What do I know about my guide of wisdom? Do I see /sense/hear my guide of wisdom's vibration? Do I see/sense/ hear what my guide of wisdom looks like? Do I see/sense /hear what my guide of wisdom is wearing? Do I see/sense/ hear a name for my guide of wisdom? Do I see/sense/hear a color or smell with my guide of wisdom?

What do I know about my doctor or healing guide? Do I see/sense/hear my doctor or healing guide's vibration? Do I see/sense/hear what my doctor or healing guide looks like? Do I see/sense/hear what my doctor or healing guide is wearing? Do I see/sense/hear a name for my doctor or healing guide? Do I see/sense/hear a color or smell with my doctor or healing guide?

What do I know about my chemist guide? Do I see/ sense/hear my chemist guide's vibration? Do I see/sense/ hear what my chemist guide looks like? Do I see/sense/hear what my chemist guide is wearing? Do I see/sense/hear a name for my chemist guide? Do I see/sense/hear a color or smell with my chemist guide?

What do I know about my psychologist guide? Do I see/sense/hear my psychologist guide's vibration? Do I see/ sense/hear what my psychologist guide looks like? Do I see/

sense/hear what my psychologist guide is wearing? Do I see/sense/hear a name for my psychologist guide? Do I see/sense/hear a color or smell with my psychologist guide?

The other guides around are your outer band of guides, master teachers and universal master teachers. The outer band of guides comes in to help you with particular lessons but may only be with you at certain times. Many reiki and tarot or divination guides are this type. Master teachers are highly evolved spirits who come in for the purpose of teaching higher lessons, and universal master teachers are the big guns, here to guide all of humanity. Universal master teachers are about the collective, so they come to teach and show us that we are all "the one" and all connected to each other. Teachers of this type are figures such as Jesus and Buddha.

I'm very lucky to work with my entourage daily (led by my gatekeeper) in addition to close work with some of my outer band guides. As mentioned earlier, I work with my reiki guides when I do reiki treatments and I have a tarot guide who helps me when I'm doing my consultations. My tarot guide came in shortly after I started to connect with my tarot deck, when I realized that working with him was what I needed to do.

As we live our lives and learn our lessons, it is important to know that there are always new outer band guides coming in to assist us. If when you are meditating and feel a new energy around you, chances are it is a new guide coming closer to you. If you use the technique above and ask questions, you should be able to connect to them and figure out what is going on.

Before I end this chapter about guides, I'd like to share a story about a master teacher, a strong and weapon-wielding one I encountered in my early days of guided meditation. As mentioned earlier, connecting to a spirit like a gatekeeper can be quite a process, something that will happen with time and practice. Strangely, my connection to this master teacher was almost instant. To this day, this master teacher is still around me and though I don't totally understand why, I'm sure she helps out when I encounter demons, negative spirits, and angry ghosts.

At the time, I had a difficult time with meditation and just couldn't get into it or stop the dead people from bugging me. Once I finally learned to relax somewhat, I found that my meditations were being pulled in a certain direction: I would always end up looking at a large statue rather than going on the journey my teacher was taking the class on. When I first saw the statue, I was taken aback—it was a huge gold statue of a woman with twelve arms. She was sitting on a tiger and had many weapons in her hands as well as a lotus flower. I had no idea who this statue was of, and guessed it was Indian or Thai.

The first time I saw that statue in meditation, I thought it was strange but merely took note of it. I wondered if it was imagination or real...and if it was my imagination, what was

I thinking? However, it kept happening the same way every week during meditation, so I started thinking there was probably more to it. Then finally, one week as I was in the meditation, I ended up in front of the statue and it looked different—beautiful bright colors. As I stood before her, she began moving. My first reaction was panic mixed with fascination as I watched her arms moving up and down like snakes. She glanced down at me, making eye contact as she began swinging some of the weapons she was holding. I thought I should just pay respect and slowly back away, but as I took small baby steps backward, she stepped off the tiger and ventured toward me, never breaking eye contact. She stood a few feet away from me, arms moving, eyes locked with mine. She then held up the lotus flower, held it out to me, and bowed. I returned the bow, not taking the flower, and opened my eyes to force myself out of the meditation. The experience was too much, and I didn't understand any of it.

When I returned home that night, I was obsessed with finding out who she was. I finally found her, eventually— her name is Durga, a Hindu goddess who was created to kill a water buffalo demon that none of the lesser gods or goddesses could kill. It is said that Durga is the source of inner power of all the gods and goddesses, who each gave a bit of their power to create her. She removes physical, mental, and spiritual pain and misery. When she laughs in the face of evil spirits, they flee, so she is considered the spirit of protection. She also provides prosperity, triumph over obstacles and enemies, and can help attain desires. There are Hindu festivals and meditations devoted especially to her. At the Durga Puja, held annually in Mahua Dham in Bihar, India, anyone afflicted or possessed by malevolent spirits, ghosts, or similar can receive healing, protection, or even an exorcism if needed.

Other students in class would see her or feel Durga's presence, and she'd show up in divinations we did in class, especially flame cards, which are blank index cards passed over a candle's flame. The smudges and burns left on the card can be interpreted for messages and omens by holding one hand over the card (do not touch it or the design will smudge), feeling what the message is, or examining the design. Every flame card I did in class had Durga on it, but she has never spoken to me. She has touched me in meditation and has given me a headdress/crown in meditation, and my mentor revealed to me in one class that she received a message that I was here to teach and fight evil, which is why I believe Durga was around me. At the time, I was stunned and remember wondering why couldn't I just get a happy gift that brings light and love? Why fighting evil? I can admit now that I'm sure it is Durga's energy that encourages me to do investigations and clearings. I realize now that evil and negativity come in many forms: ignorance, hatred, cruelty, and the like. Giving people the tools to connect to themselves and each other eliminates and destroys evil. When I hear of a nasty entity tormenting a family or business, I don't get intimidated—I get energized to go and kick butt.

Durga's energy is probably why many of the nastier ghosts stay clear of me as well. One client who visited me for a reading had a cousin who took his own life and became a nasty, angry ghost. He would not come in the room with us but stayed behind the basement door, actually crushing some plastic bins during our session. We were talking about him, and I could feel him—the more I discussed him and the negative influence he had on the client, the angrier he became. He knew I was teaching her to protect herself from his energy. Suddenly, we heard a huge crash in my basement. I ran downstairs and found that three rubber bins had been crushed on one end, tipping and spilling their contents all over the floor. However, the ghost was nowhere to be seen, and it really made me angry. I demanded he come out, but he did not. For the rest of the reading, the ghost stomped up and down the basement stairs making as much noise as possible to scare his cousin, but he would not come near me. I think Durga's energy was more responsible in this case, but I'm grateful she shares it with me.

Most times when I meditate, Durga sits in front of me at rest, looking like she is also meditating, I am truly grateful and will never take her for granted. I'm blessed to have this master teacher around me so often, and her gift of the lotus flower is the main reason I named my company Purple Lotus. The lotus is also a symbol of growth and overcoming adversity, so I'm honored to have received this gift from this master teacher.

10

Receiving Messages

I lower myself into the hot water of my tub, submerging my shoulders and taking in a deep breath to clear the tension I often carry in my body. Closing my eyes, I lie back and relax each muscle in my body. Ah, a wonderful and rare brief moment of peace! As I relax, I start to see flashes of people and objects. My moment of peace was just that—a moment. As I accept the fact that I might be able to shut down the physical world for a moment, closing the door to my busy life, I will never be able to shut down my connection to the other side. I should know better; water and quiet just don't mix in my world. The symbols, feelings, and messages flow while water is around, to say nothing of being submerged in it.

I have received some of the clearest messages for myself and others while taking a bath or shower, but I have also had moments where I was so overwhelmed with messages flying at me that I couldn't make out anything. Those are usually the

149

times when I refuse to listen. I still hear it all—I just turn my back to it, and sometimes even if the message is clear and not overwhelming, I often get pulled into life and ignore the messages or doubt what I'm receiving. I always say to my clients and my loved ones that there is a *huge* difference between hearing dead people and listening to dead people.

This chapter is very complicated for me to write, as the topic is so simple yet so complicated. And as serious and technical as it is, it is also amazing and inspirational. To start, not all messages from the other side are straightforward and not all messages are clear. Even for me, there are times I clearly hear a message like "turn left," leaving little doubt about the message's contents but then I receive other messages as symbols or signs. Sometimes I receive them in meditation or dreams, or may even meet someone who delivers me the message. An example of this is when I decided (actually thought I should but didn't really do anything) to give yoga a try. A friend came to do an exchange reading (when two or more people exchange services, a reading for a reading). During my session, she said that for many reasons I needed to do yoga; it would help me physically and spiritually—this was message one. The next day, I met with a client who said she was a yogi, a master of yoga—message two. I remember thinking as she was telling me about what she does for a living that there seemed to be a yoga theme in my life, but I ignored it as I like to do. A few days passed and then stuck in my door I found a card announcing that a new yoga studio was opening in my neighborhood—message three. I actually laughed at how obvious these messages were as I threw the card into the recycle bin. I finally got the message, loud and clear!

I consider myself a skeptic or a realist, not one of those spiritual people who thinks everything is a message. Everything happens for a reason, yes, but some things are simply what they appear to be—nothing more, nothing less. When you find a penny or a dime, it may be that someone ahead of you dropped it and you're the lucky person who found it... there may not be a bigger message. However, if you find dimes constantly, I'd say someone is trying to get your attention. On the opposite end of things is the biggest mistake of all—analyzing messages to death. Trust me, we do not need to analyze every single message; we just need to be aware and in the now. Like I've said, the universe and dead people will make it clear when the time is right so we just need to thank them and continue to be aware of signs. The usual rule is that if you see something three times, it is a clear message. So if you hear a song that reminds you of your mother who is on the other side and then hear it two more times in a row, chances are she is around you.

After years of hearing and not listening to messages, my main advice to clients and students is to ask questions and always be aware and in the now. Sounds crazy I know, but if you want to know if there is more to a sign or message, ask! If you hear that song that reminds you of your mother, ask her,

"If you have more to say to me other than hello, please give me another sign or point me in the direction I should go." Trust me that if a spirit wants to say something, they will. It really does come down to trusting and paying attention. The universe, our guides, and our loved ones on the other side are always working to put things in our path to guide us in the right direction. We call it coincidence, but remember there is no such thing as coincidence—it is synchronicity!

Really, messages are just ways for us to be guided down our path, moving through the ebbs and flows easier. For those out there who have no clue what I'm talking about, it's simple: our path is our life, what we are here to do and learn. The ebbs and flows are the bad and good times we all have. To know that we are being helped and are really never alone is a huge comfort. We can let go of fear and worry, as neither help us—they only slow us down and prevent us from seeing messages. Think of messages as the GPS of life—let it help you navigate.

I understand that not all of us are mediums or psychics, but as I've said many times I do feel we all have some form of intuition. We can all learn to listen to the GPS, even if the loudest it gets is a whisper or a feeling. You may not hear the equivalent of a honking horn like I do, but hearing is possible. For those who really want to hone their message receiving, there are different techniques explained later.

One of the first things to figure out is how you receive messages. There are many ways to do that, but I believe the easiest is developmental mediation (see chapter 8), as it is the best way to figure out how you receive a message—scent, symbols, words, whole stories, or feelings. We all receive in different ways, so how we receive is as important as what we receive. Developmental mediation quiets the world around us, leaving just us and our guides and loved ones free to connect.

When I was learning in a circle or class, the main way we'd hone our message receiving was through the use of billets. Everyone took a small square piece of blank paper, wrote a question on it, then signed the paper. Some methods have you write the names of three loved ones—the dead people you'd hope would come in to answer the question—and three master teachers' names as well. The paper was then folded so no one could see anyone's question or signature. Each person also drew a picture on the front to identify it as theirs, and then it was placed in a basket. When everyone was finished, the basket was passed around and everyone took one billet, making sure to not take their own (that's what the picture is for). When everyone had one in hand, it was held while doing a guided meditation. A fun and interesting test is to meditate without a billet. The meditation should remain neutrally focused, but chances are it will be different when holding a billet, connected to whomever the billet belongs to. When finished with the meditation, everyone shared what messages they received. These exercises were no-pressure, so it was fine if someone didn't receive anything. Receiving something was pretty common, however, and people reported receiving messages in lots of different forms such as feelings—the billet could be hot or cold, tingly or calm, or make the person holding it feel sick or hyper. All of those sensations can be messages, so all we needed to do was be aware while letting go.

I consider the process of receiving messages like this to be like watching television or a movie where you are simply observing and being aware. If you do see something, make sure you get all the details. Is there a certain color standing out? If there is water, is it calm or stormy? All these things can be messages. When coming out of a meditation to give your messages, never add to what you received; only give what you get, even if it makes zero sense to you.

One fun thing to add as you get comfortable with group-style receiving is seeing if you can tell who the billet belongs to before showing the symbol on the front. Are you pulled to a certain person or can you tell by the message you received during the meditation who it belongs to? It's even possible to receive their name.

Doing group developmental mediations are a wonderful way to get confirmation about what you receive. You may get something that makes no sense to you or the owner of the billet and then the next time the group is together, the person may bring you confirmation that happened after the fact. I've seen this happen over and over again.

The other more obvious way to get messages is through divination, of which there are quite a few methods. I break down a few of the most common ones at the end of this chapter. The use of a divination can help not only confirm a message you are receiving but it will also help you with letting go and connecting to the spirits around you and the universe. My number one piece of advice is always the same: *no* meditation or divination will work if you do not let go. You need to just let it happen, relax, and let it flow. Once you put any pressure on it, you will not receive properly. It either will not come at all or you will end up putting your interpretation into it. You need to check your ego at the door and just let go. I teach my students this but see and feel them starting to put pressure on themselves. They are so determined to give something that the pressure they applied to it makes them unable to receive. I was able to show students how to let go because I experienced it firsthand. If a student would say, "I only get a star," I'd correct them immediately and say, "You are getting a star, not 'only,'" then as the class went on and they were listening to others giving messages, they would relax and end up getting a ton more messages.

There really is no room for ego, and we need to learn to accept what we get. If it is wrong, it's wrong, no big deal. The more you practice, the more clear the message will come. Let go and trust what you receive. If you get a purple gorilla wearing a pink bikini, then that's what you say. It may seem silly or irrelevant to you, but to the person receiving the message it may mean a great deal. As the reader or person picking up the message, you are often not meant to know the meaning, only the message; the meaning is for the person receiving the message, not the messenger.

When you put pressure on yourself to receive a message, you can use your own energy to receive; this can be really depleting. I did not understand how this worked until my mentor strongly urged me to take reiki. She didn't tell me why it was important that I take reiki, only that I should. After taking a reiki level 1 class, it all made sense. I could see how I was pulling from my own energy, and once I allowed the dead people's messages to just flow through me, similar to reiki energy, I went from being exhausted after having two client sessions to being able to see many clients and feel more energized with each one. Reiki taught me the important lesson that it is better to be a screen rather than a sponge, especially as an empath; energy should flow through us rather than be sapped or stuck to us.

I wish everyone could receive messages in words; it would make life so much easier. One student of mine is quite lucky—he receives messages like on a Telex machine (for youngsters or anyone out there who has no idea what a Telex is, it's like a very old computer), so it "types" across his mind. Usually, dead people are not as straightforward with their messages; if they are not speaking like Yoda, they show symbols or stories. Deciphering their symbols can be challenging, and the only true way to understand meanings is to write down the symbol and any details, and see what happens. I often tell my clients a red rose to me is love and passion but to someone else may mean death or blood.

A number of years ago, I was meditating and received a very detailed story: my husband's boss at the time was greeted by Death as a hooded giant (at least nine feet tall) with a sickle. I stood watching as Death in all his giant glory slowly moved toward my husband's boss, only stopping when he was half an arm's length away. They stood and glared at each other until Death banged his sickle on the ground. Sparks flew everywhere, and then everything went black. I jumped out of my mediation freaking out and wondering why they were showing me this. I immediately called my mentor asking for advice: "Do I tell him I received a message that he was going to die? Death had his address and was coming to call!" She calmly said, "Lisa, write down the message and see what happens. That is all you can do. If he is meant to die, you can't stop it, nor should you." I wrote it down and then watched the meaning unfold a few months later. Steve's boss was leading the life of the ultimate bachelor until he met someone with whom he quickly fell in love. He more or less stopped his partying ways, got married—a thing he swore he would never do—and started a family. His life was turned inside out and transformed; the old version was dead and he was living a new life. I know now that when I see Death in a meditation, the meaning is similar to the Death card of tarot—rebirth and transformation, or the "death" of a way of being and not actually dying. So Death had the man's address and did come a-callin' but not in the way I thought.

Learning the meaning of messages is a process; you need to be patient—and I can't believe I said that because I definitely struggle with patience at times (one of my life lessons). It is also important to be responsible in your message giving. Consider my husband's boss example—if I were to give my husband's boss that message as is, wow... what could it have done to him? I shudder when I think about how I could have scared him and his family. I know I said to give what you get, but we should never give messages when they are not asked for. When my clients come to see me, they are giving me permission to give them messages, so in that context I give what I get. Ethics and responsibility are just as important when giving messages, so if I do receive something I find disturbing, I ask the dead people for more detail before relaying the message. As I've been doing this a long time and have worked very hard at learning how I receive and interpret the dead people, I take it very seriously and teach my students to be the same. Message giving is not something to take lightly.

I recently had an experience with another medium I met while out and about. I was with a group of people I know who are acquaintances, not close personal friends. We started chatting about general stuff like the weather when this person started to read me in front of everyone.

I was horrified! She blurted out information that was only half correct though I do think she has a gift—she revealed the fact that I was working on this book. Here's the thing, though: I was *not* ready or willing to share that information with anyone, especially acquaintances. I was very uncomfortable, and it drove home in a painful way why no one should ever give messages unless asked. I make exceptions if I receive an extremely strong and important message for someone, in which case I pull them aside and ask if I may give it to them. I'd say 99.9 percent of the time I will tell the dead people to bring the person they have the message for to me in private, as they have the power to do that.

The other thing with receiving and giving messages is responsibility. I teach that we give what we get, but as someone who is giving the messages, you need to get as much information as possible before delivering anything. If a spirit tells me "everything is going to be okay," I instantly ask: "Spirit 'okay' or living 'okay'" because they can be very different. If an experience is going to lead to a huge life lesson or a major upheaval in life and is "meant" to happen, spirit nearly celebrates with a party—they think it is fantastic because they know we will learn and grow from the experience and will ultimately be okay and most likely in a better place afterward. For us, the experience can be horrible. It could feel like the furthest thing from "okay" until we are through it and realize it was probably the best thing for us. During the struggle, however, we don't always see it that way.

I have seen and cringed many times watching others deliver messages irresponsibly to people, seemingly not realizing a message has the ability to empower or crush someone. At a dinner party once, one guest in the group was a medium, so another woman mentioned she was having dreams and kept seeing the number 52. Her father was fifty-two years old and was going on a motorcycle trip to Las Vegas, so she was worried that Spirit was giving her a message that something was going to happen to him. This other medium spoke up and said, "I keep seeing the word 'yes,' so something *is* going to happen to him." This angered me because I could see the woman's face pale as every scenario ran through her head, all involving some sort of tragedy. Though I was sitting quietly, I couldn't bear to watch what was happening; it was cruel. I spoke up and explained that the word "something" is pretty open and could mean anything—"something" could mean he was going to win a jackpot; it could mean he would meet the love of his life and get married; it means a million different potential things and scenarios of which only a few are bad. If she wanted to ask Spirit a question about her dad, she should ask for details, for specifics. "Is my father going to be safe on his trip?" or "Is my father going to have a wonderful time on his trip?" in this case would have been way more productive than "Is he going to be okay?" or "Is something going to happen?" The latter two questions are way too open—they can mean anything. The other medium said, "Well something is going to happen—I can feel it!" I agreed: "Something is *always* happening. It's happening right now, and every second of every day 'something' is happening. The birds are singing, the sun is shining, and we are having this conversation. So you're right … 'something' will happen."

People who are blessed with psychic and medium gifts are here to help, guide, empower, and comfort. We are just tools for the dead people and the universe, so it is really about the message—not us and what we can do that others can't.

Message receiving is about being able to walk our paths as best as we can without becoming stuck in the ebbs or trapped with a fear of moving forward. It is not about the future and what may or may not happen. Messages guide us in life but shouldn't tell us our destination. After all, looking to the far future is not a good way to live. If we are too busy looking in that direction, we end up missing the incredible things in the now—those lessons, signs, and opportunities that move us toward the amazing life we want and deserve. Messages can aid us to confidently make decisions in the present, but we should always balance messages using the head, the heart, and intuition. As I've said many times, that balance is key. We need to live, learn, and trust. We can use message receiving and giving as a tool to do just that, but we must remember it is just a tool. Our gifts can help us be aware of synchronicity, our connection to the universe and each other, but it can't stop there.

Most people want to know the future, what will be. Well here's the thing about that: you may receive a message about the future and it could definitely give you hope, but if you do not live in the now and do what needs to be done now, that message could likely be pushed further and further away. And if we knew the future, would we walk our paths the same way? I really do not think so. One of my favorite quotes on the matter comes from *The Matrix*, and it states that "there is a difference between knowing your path and walking your path." Each of us must still take a step before arriving at the future, and without those steps the future may change or stay the future. I believe that some things are destiny; if something is meant to happen, it will and the matter becomes when. That "when" is determined by those steps and lessons we learn. Basically, in order for something to happen, we may have to experience other things before it can happen.

Some of my friends and clients go to other psychics and mediums and are told wonderful, amazing things, and I don't doubt there's an amount of truth to their messages. Unfortunately, receiving nothing but incredible and out-of-this-world uplifting words tends to make people wait, which in turn makes the future wait. I've seen people receive messages about winning the lottery, and instead of working their butts off (walking their path) to make their life prosperous on their own and following the opportunities the universe places in front of them, they sit and wait for that message to come true. Well, what *if* you are to win the lottery and the message was correct *but* you are supposed to achieve a level of personal successes before it happens? Maybe you needed to learn something before being handed a large sum of money or you needed to meet certain people. Until the synchronicity happens, the lottery win will not happen either. Sitting and waiting for that jackpot to land in your lap stops your life from flowing. You wouldn't be walking your path.

Message receiving was once explained to me by one of my closest friends as a full glass of water being dumped into an open hand. The message receiver only catches a few drops of that message as we are not privy to the big picture, only receiving a small portion the universe feels we can use to guide us to our fullest life. We are not meant to know the destination, we are to live life. Message receiving and divinations are tools we can use to confirm that we are on track, but remember to always balance it. Body, Mind, and Soul!

As I mentioned earlier in this chapter, divinations are a great way to receive messages. I love divinations! Divinations are tools that people have used for centuries to connect to Spirit or the universe. There are many but the most common are tarot, dowsing, and psychometry.

When I was new to divination, I tried many different forms and encourage my students and clients to do the same. Start with the types you find most interesting or attractive and then go from there. My friend and I used to hold divination Fridays where we'd get together and try a different one. You can't master a divination method in a day, but you can get a feel for it and see if you want to continue to learn and practice it.

Tarot is divination using cards, and luckily there are many, many gorgeous decks out there now. Once you get into reading cards, it is hard to own just one tarot deck. I own a bunch of tarot decks and actually have to stop myself from buying more.

My advice when it comes to tarot is to find a deck that really speaks to you, one that you connect with, and when you touch the cards and lay them out, they almost seem to talk to you plainly or clearly. When I teach tarot, I always tell my students to read the book that comes with the deck exactly once and then put the book aside. Next, look at the cards. What do they say to you? What do you see in a card? Once you have spent time with the cards, you can start to learn different spreads.

After laying the cards out in a spread, attempt to read without the book. When you have finished, pick up the book and see if they are similar—chances are they will be. If not, remember that divination is a practice of letting go and allowing information to flow through you. It is a fabulous way to connect to the universe and your abilities.

Dowsing has to be one of my favorite divinations not only because of how correct it is but also the reaction I receive from clients when they first see it work. Dowsing rods can either be two L-shaped rods or one in a Y shape.

The L rods are made out of copper and brass and the Y is usually a strong yet bendable wood. There are other forms out there but these are the basic and most common. You don't have to buy anything fancy, especially when starting. A friend and I made our first sets of L rods out of two wire coat hangers. Cut and bend them to form an L. These worked amazingly for me, but people often questioned me while using them because they thought I was somehow doing a magic trick and turning them with my fingers. The pair I use currently has outer handles that allow the rods to spin freely when held.

When some people first start using rods, they find they need to walk slowly to get the rods to work, so if you are standing still and don't get any activity, try walking around until you get something.

Most people have heard of dowsing for water, and in fact some people still use dowsers when drilling for a well. For us spiritual-minded people, dowsing can be done for answers or confirmation of answers. Each time before working with rods for an answer, be sure to ask the rods: "Will you work with me? Show me a yes. Now show me a no." Depending on the spirit you are working with, they may move differently. Some spirits I work with use the rods opening as a yes and others the rods crossing as a yes. It is very important to ask each time.

If you decide to learn dowsing and purchase rods, my advice is to practice with them first before asking questions.

Walk around your house. If you pass directly over water, the rods should cross. If they don't, keep practicing. When teaching dowsing, the example I use is passing the rods over my dog's water bowl or sink, demonstrating how they cross.

Important note: When dowsing for answers, make sure all liquid is either behind you or not near you at all. Dowsing and boats do not mix! A few students once told me they couldn't get their rods to work. When I asked how they were doing it, most of them told me they sat down at their table with their coffee and started asking questions. Either their rods went nuts or stayed crossed. Well, the liquid in their mug was messing it all up. Once they removed the liquid, things improved.

The next practice after finding liquid/water is to use the rods to find missing items. Have someone in your house hide your keys or another item. Picture the item in your mind and then follow the rods. They will point in the direction you need to walk in. Be sure you walk slowly and allow the rods to change their direction. When you do get to the location, the rods will cross when you have found the item.

I have used my rods to find many missing items for friends and clients. I have gone to farms to locate missing iPods in hay mazes and missing jewelry in clients' homes. I have also used dowsing rods to locate spirit or ghosts in locations when I can feel but cannot see them.

Psychometry is the ability to pick up on energy from an item, reading its history and energy. It is very similar to the residual energy mentioned in the energy chapter. For some people, it also allows you to connect to the person whether they are living or dead. I always find psychometry interesting and love the feeling of being able to connect to an item. To focus my energy on an item and be able to get a story from someone's past and feel what that person felt is incredible.

Empaths are usually naturally very gifted at psychometry. Because they can already pick up energy from many items, psychometry is a great practice for empaths to give them practice with separating, feeling, and reading different energies—is the energy positive or negative? Is it telling a story? Psychometry also helps empaths learn to separate from different energies, putting it aside and brushing off others' energy as well.

To sense energy with psychometry, hold the item in your hand. Many people say you receive with your left hand, but I find it is different for all of us so test both. As you learn, you'll discover which is best for you. Once you have the item in hand, pay attention to everything you are feeling. Does the item feel hot or cold, and is the temperature changing as you hold the item? Does the item feel positive or negative? You can hold the item to your third eye as well to pick up any information. Maybe you can see symbols, images, people, places, or items. What you will see mostly depends on how you receive messages. If you receive in words, you may hear information about the item in question. For empaths or people who pick up feelings, holding the item to your solar-plexus chakra will increase the information you can receive, especially when learning.

If you try psychometry, there are a couple things to keep in mind: one, you need to brush your aura off once you are finished reading an item. You are stepping into another energy and allowing your body to absorb whatever is coming through the item, so always remember to remove it! Also remember that the energy on an item could be mixed with the person who handed it over to you to read. An example of this is if a client wants you to read a ring that belonged to her mother who passed away but the client wears the ring every day. The ring's energy could have a combination of both the mother's and the client's energy... or even just the client's energy. I always recommend that when someone brings me an item to read whether the item belonged to a dead or living person, it must be handled with care, such as putting the item in a bag and handling it as little as possible.

If psychometry comes easily to you, please remember that any item brought into your home will have energy that you can easily sense. If someone was angry with you when they bought the gift they are giving you now, their negative energy could be on the item. If you purchase something made in a factory where conditions are not great or the person who made the item has bad energy, that energy can be on the item. You must cleanse everything. I realized this when I bought mala beads in Chinatown; I'd bring them home and start feeling sad or negative. I threw out many strands of beads before I realized I could just cleanse them. What I do now before I purchase anything is feel the energy coming off of it. If it is really horrible, I do not purchase it. If the energy is okay, I cleanse it. I cleanse the item using different techniques, depending on what the item is. If it is small, I put it on a windowsill for a few days to allow the sun and moon to cleanse the energy from it. Larger items I smudge using sage or incense or I use reiki on the item. You should do the same thing for gifts that come into your home.

Besides divination and meditation, I also believe channeling and remote viewing are two methods that are important to discuss. Mediums and psychics can easily channel, and there are a couple different types of channeling, all of which are covered in the next chapter. The other form is remote viewing, which is similar to astral traveling but not quite identical.

Remote viewing is the ability to be in one location and see another place or person in the mind, experiencing and seeing exactly what is happening at the moment of viewing. With remote viewing, you are able to think of a person or place and go there remotely. You can see what the person is doing and what is happening in the location, similar to astral travel. I have never astral traveled so I'm unable to explain the difference in my own words. However, what I understand from people who do astral travel is that you are sending your astral body out while in a meditative state, separating from your other body while attached by a cord. At least for me, remote viewing is more a mental state. I project my energy or mind to that person or place, and in some situations (most, actually) it feels like being a ghost or spirit. I can move around a space and see everything around me, as if I was there physically.

I actually didn't know that this ability had a name until my mentor called me after taking a course herself on remote viewing a number of years ago. She explained it and I was shocked because I just naturally do this! At first I didn't really realize what I was doing. I'd just think of a person and see them at home or work, as well as any items around them and I could even feel how they were feeling or the energy in the place they were. I thought I was imagining it all, until I'd talk to them and they'd tell me something they were doing that day. At first I thought it was a psychic thing, like I was seeing the future (something I never have been able to do), but then I started to become aware of doing it consciously when doing reiki and cord-cutting meditations. Cords are emotional attachments sent from other people that can be positive, negative, or even controlling. I'd be able to find cords attached to myself or my client and then follow that cord to the person who attached it. I'd then be able to watch and follow that person. It was an effective way to cut the cord and stop it from reattaching and causing issues. The only downside is that I would soon feel the person's physical ailments like heartburn or feeling hung over or drunk.

There's nothing like feeling any of those feeling when you've not had any of the fun to receive them!

Once my mentor and I discussed remote viewing, she added it to her class, which was an amazing opportunity for me to put it to the test. She'd direct us to a person by giving us the location, street address, or intersection. She'd then let us roam the property remotely and not tell us a thing about who lived there and what was happening. After each exercise, I realized how natural this was for me. Not only could I see everything and feel the person, I could also pick up on residual energy. I could see what took place before. It wasn't far in the past, but it was enough to help me solve the issues within the location and tell a client what was happening.

I use remote viewing techniques when I do photo psychometry: I feel their energy, step into them, and/or watch them using remote viewing. Otherwise, I try my best not to remote view without people's permission. I only use it when a client asks or comes to me for reiki with big issues and I need help to solve them. Remote viewing is a fine line to walk as it is very intrusive. If you have permission, it can be very fun to do.

There are a few ways of practicing remote viewing. The first is with yourself when sitting down to meditate and going through your body to relax and balance your chakras. While doing these other exercises, you can also scan your body to see if any cords are attached to you. We all have cords attached to us; some are good—they are bright and

balanced, usually from our children and healthy relationships. If any are dark and thick, they should be removed
because these cords can make you feel ill or negative, and
they can pull your energy or put thoughts into it. Before you
remove any of the negative cords, you can follow them and
see where they take you. Can you see a person on the other
end? Why is this person attaching this cord? Jealousy, anger,
or fear? From there, you can then remotely feel the person's
energy and what they are doing. Don't stay too long—let it
go, come back, and cut the cord. You want to free your body
from the negative energy being sent to you. I find the longer
I hang out in this manner with the person, the more I come
back with their emotions and physical issues.

You can do the same when doing reiki on a client. After
balancing their energy, look for any cords and follow them. It
is very helpful because the client may be feeling out of sorts. By
giving them information about why a cord was attached, it will
help them to prevent it from reattaching. For you, the person
practicing remote viewing, it is interesting to be able to follow
a cord to someone you do not know, explain to the client what
the person looks like and where they may be.

Another way of practicing is with a friend. Together,
decide on a date and time. Make the person aware that you
are going to remote view them, and after you have visited
them, call the person and confirm whether what you were
seeing and feeling was correct. At first you may only see
small things but as you practice more, a lot more detail will

come forward. When my mentor was practicing this, she remote viewed a friend. She saw her friend sitting in a chair with a book, and behind her was a boat. After the session, she called her friend and told her what she had picked up. What she found out was that the friend was indeed sitting in a chair reading but wasn't near a boat … but beside her on the wall was a large painting of a boat. So my mentor was right, but she just didn't see that it was a painting; she thought her friend was outside near a boat. The more she practiced, the clearer the details became.

I have taught remote viewing in my class, and the experience was quite interesting. The first time, I had my students sit quietly. I instructed them to mentally walk through my front door, go up the stairs into my daughter's bedroom, and then after letting them check out her room for a moment, leave. The results were incredible—a couple of the students were accurate in what they saw remotely, even though they didn't understand what they were seeing and thought it must be wrong. At the time I did this exercise, my daughter had painted her room purple with polka dots all on the walls. A couple students just saw purple, and one saw purple as well as what she described as white orbs all over the room. She thought she was seeing a lot of spirits in the room when actually it was just white polka dots. With more practice, she would definitely have been able to pick up much more detail.

Remote viewing is sometimes used as a method to locate missing people. Personally, I have never attempted it; I think you'd have to be really good at letting go of the emotions and be able to look at the location to get information. You'd have to be able to connect to the person, see their location and how they are feeling, and hope you give information that will lead to their recovery.

Many people believe remote viewing is extra sensory perception (ESP) and I suppose it is. However, these days the term has become a substitute for "psychic," and "ESP" is similarly a label that includes many gifts—it's a generalization. People who don't know the difference between a psychic or a medium lump it all together as "psychic" or "ESP."

Channeling

Like many mediums, I could easily allow a spirit or ghost to use my body as a channel. There have been many occasions when a spirit or ghost has attempted to do such a thing to me, but I put my foot down and did not allow it. When a spirit attempts to do this, it is called over-shadowing. It is the strangest feeling, like a person is physically sitting on you. Your body becomes heavy and it is hard to move your arms or legs, almost like being held down.

There are two types of channeling: semi-trance and trance state. Semi-trance is when the medium is awake and aware of what is going on. The medium remembers everything that is said, and they actively allow the spirit to sit over them and use their body and voice as a tool. Although the medium is aware, they relinquish control and allow the spirit control for the moment.

In a full trance, the dead person enters the body and the medium is not aware of what is happening. The medium will not remember what is said or how long they have been in the trance.

Like with other gifts, some people are natural channels. These people must learn to have control of their gifts, if not it can really disrupt their lives. I have had a number of debates with a few of my colleagues about how I do readings and many believe that what I do is a form of a semi-trance channeling. I do not think it is, because to me channeling involves the dead person physically entering your body and taking over your thoughts and movements. I do not allow the dead people to physically enter my body; I speak to them using my third eye and then pass on the information. I'm also always fully aware of what I say. Others think a semi-trance does not require the dead person to enter your body, but I disagree. I do often say things I would never think to say and typically don't remember what has been discussed in a session once it's over. I may remember the client and a few minor comments but for the most part I don't, which to many mediums means a semi-trance state. They have good points but I'm being stubborn and not willing to admit it is a form of channeling. I have seen a few people channel, and what I do is not similar.

My mentor channels on occasion, going into a complete trance. I have sat and watched as she invited the spirit to enter her body, and it's freaky—her whole being changes. The first time it happened was quite uncomfortable to watch; it wasn't that I was frightened of the dead person, it was more about control. Many "what ifs" ran through my head as I watched her do it the first time: What if the dead person didn't leave her body? What if she couldn't push them out?

My mentor's class typically has ten to twelve people in it, and these types of meditation classes (or what others in the spiritual world call a circle) usually have seats arranged in a circle. This is done for many reasons, but mainly it is to raise the vibration and be protected as everyone within the circle links their energy around each other. This practice is incredibly helpful, especially when first starting out. Receiving messages is easier in a circle than when doing it solo.

Normally, my mentor would turn off all the lights so we'd meditate in complete darkness, but one night she left a lamp on. After guiding us through a meditation, she said that a spirit was bugging her to channel, so she would do it. The room was normally quiet but on this night it seemed to still completely, as if everyone in the room was holding their breath or stuck in freeze frame. I watched as she took a few deep breaths and then slowly it happened. She changed the position she was sitting in and straightened her back, and her appearance seemed different, changed. Her nose seemed wider and larger, as did her lips. It was clear to me that we were now looking at someone other than my mentor. I thought at first it was just the lighting, so I swiveled in my seat to look directly at her, thinking if I looked from another angle I'd realize it was just my eyes playing a trick on me. But as I moved, her head slowly turned in my direction. Her eyes remained closed but it was as if she could see me. The spirit was giving me a good look that squashed any doubt. If anything, I just had more questions and was freaked out completely.

Slowly turning back to the others in the circle, the spirit my mentor was channeling spoke. The voice that came out was like none I have ever heard before—soft yet firm, and with a hint of an echo. The spirit spoke about things I've heard many dead people talk about, such as the universe and how we are all connected, that we are all one and whatever we do to each other we really do to ourselves. It was all very spiritual and what I call "big picture" stuff that the average person doesn't really care about. After about ten minutes of this, my mentor's shoulders dropped, and I knew the spirit had left her body. She came to blinking and a little out of it. She had no idea what the spirit had said or how long it had been in her.

At the time of my mentor's channeling, I had been active with that group for about five years and had never witnessed her do that before. As interesting as it was, I hoped to never witness it again and I swore in that moment that I'd never go down that road myself as I'm a bit of a control freak about these things. Sure, I learned to let go and let the information come through me instead of fighting it, but I do not consider it channeling; instead it's like the dead people plug into my third eye and I use my mouth as the speaker—I'm not going to let someone else take over my body.

About six months after my mentor channeled in class, she taught us automatic writing. Although this technique is more of a divination, I think it's a form of channeling, as it allows the dead people to take over your body. This technique of receiving messages is extremely interesting, but it requires the medium/sensitive to completely let go and allow the dead people to take over an arm and hand to write the message. My first attempt felt almost like arm wrestling with the dead—they were all excited and wanted to use my hand but I did not let go and was not willing to allow it. The only thing on the paper was a few random scribbles. After a few weeks of practicing the technique, I let go a tiny bit and allowed a dead person to use my hand. It was completely creepy. I know my issue is giving over the control I want and the dead people needing it to communicate this way. In some ways it is a little silly—I can feel and/or see the dead person standing beside me and can usually speak with them freely. Yet giving up use of my hand to a dead person and feeling it move without my mind telling it to move is strange and uncomfortable.

If you are going to learn automatic writing, you must protect yourself and truly let go. Some people say they can do auto writing but usually they are either receiving a message in their third eye and writing it down, or they are using their own feelings to write out a message. Neither is auto writing, as auto writing is truly allowing dead people to take over the hand and use it to write out a message. You'll know it's working when you have no mental control over your hand—you could be thinking about your grocery list but your hand is writing a message about what's going to happen to you next week.

One of the scariest situations I have ever witnessed related to allowing dead people to take control of a body involved a fellow student in my mentor's class. This woman was so weak-minded, she was terrified about everything. She was such a quivering bag of bones most days that dead people used her like a plaything. She held on to her fear like a life raft, yet it was the one thing hurting her the most. She would tell us stories of the dead people she'd run into, no different than what I lived with before setting boundaries. Actually, I think she didn't see them as often as I do. Instead of wanting to learn to either control it or use it to enhance herself, she just stayed in the fear. My mentor told her over and over again how important it was to come out of that fear and take control, but she wouldn't listen.

This woman was so not in control of her own body that she would be taken over by dead people constantly. She'd be at work or out shopping and a ghost/spirit would enter her and she would go into a trance and be completely unaware of her actions. There were times when she'd get on a bus or train and end up hours away from where she worked and lived. She'd come to not knowing how she got there or why. In class she was constantly being taken over, to the point where the class's attention was pulled to focus on her and her issues. I was never sure if she was just creating drama or what until one night about four months after my mother-in-law passed away. We had just started meditation when this woman started to make little noises. My mentor asked if she was okay and the woman announced in a Scottish accent that she "wasn't happy with Lisa." I was completely shocked because this lady was Italian with an Italian accent—to hear the change in her voice threw me off guard. I knew immediately it was my mother-in-law, the last person I ever expected to come through. This woman started talking to me exactly like my mother-in-law would have, saying things that only my mother-in-law would have known. I realized in that moment that whatever was happening to this woman was really happening... and she also enjoyed the attention it gave her. Between her anxieties and finally getting attention, she had no desire to become strong, stop this madness, and learn to control her gift. Recently, I ran into a close friend of hers and was very saddened to hear that nothing had changed for the woman. In fact, she had actually become worse, alienating herself from some family and friends because she would not stop being afraid and take control.

Channeling cannot happen unless you invite spirits in or you are weak of mind. For this reason, mediums need to be cautious about taking drugs and alcohol. When most people drink alcohol, the chakras open completely or at least wider than normal, allowing many things to affect them. Although some senses are slower, some are heightened. When a medium drinks alcohol or does drugs, the two main chakras used to connect to the other side—the third eye and crown chakras—become so open that we cannot control who or what enters us.

As mentioned in an earlier chapter I always tell my students (especially young ones) that moderation is key. If you are going to drink and weaken your abilities to control your gifts, you need to be careful. Drinking or doing drugs widens our third eye so large that it goes from being a home satellite dish to the size of the Arecibo Observatory (that gigantic dish in Puerto Rico). In that state, it's likely you'll end up reading everyone, getting messages and saying things you shouldn't. You may end up seeing things you shouldn't, no longer in control to stop the bad energies. For any mediums or sensitives out there reading this, please be careful. Moderation is necessary.

If you are a natural channel, it can be wonderful and rewarding once you learn to hone it. Channelers I know always deliver the most amazing messages, and after speaking to many of them, they have all told me the same thing— honing this skill is the same as any. You must practice, practice, practice!

······················ **12** ······················

Top Lessons I've Learned from Dead People

Over the years, I have learned so many things from dead people; I feel truly blessed that information can flow through me and that I can share it with clients. Many times, messages for clients are similar but presented in different ways.

What follows is not in any specific order, and as I'm writing these I'm overcome with just how important some of these messages from Spirit are. Some are very straight-forward, and others only seem that way but actually have a bit of complexity to them. I'll try my best to make them easy to understand. They are important, and I'm truly honored to be able to learn these valuable lessons and pass them on.

Grief

When it comes to grief, all dead people (with the exception of ghosts) say the same thing: Life is to be lived! Dead people do not want us to grieve for long. They understand we are humans with emotions and must grieve. It is not good to ignore or suppress your feelings, but neither can we allow them to control or consume us. To that end, if Spirit had their way, we'd mourn for a day or two, or a week, tops. They want us to remember them and embrace those memories, not pull away in pain (which is almost an insult to their memory, according to them). They do not want us to suffer, no matter what their circumstances were; they want us to grab on to life and live! They understand the physical loss, but to their thinking they can be with us *more* on the other side. They know that not everyone can see or talk to them, but they guide us in their own way and tell us they are around in many different ways, if only we would stop mourning and pay attention. We could even detect them as a particular scent or song that tells us they are with us. They are never far away.

An important lesson I have learned regarding the presence of our departed ones is in cases where their energy upsets you. You often can feel them around you or see them in dreams, but if you haven't let go and moved on past their death, they will step back. They may still come in and watch but they will not come close because they do not want to hurt us. I see this kind of distance often when people do not move forward. They come to me and say they used to feel the person's energy around them but don't any longer. Why would someone stay around you if they are clearly causing you pain? If you want them to guide and be around you, let go and live. They want us to be all we can be, not watch us get stuck because of their death. Letting go is a life lesson, one that we should all know is necessary and important. We want to honor our loved ones who have passed by not holding onto them.

If for some reason your loved one hasn't crossed over and is a ghost, realize that holding on and mourning them will hold them here longer. It is best to send them in death to the other side, knowing that they will be fine and happy, never too far away from you.

There is No Bad

There's no such thing as bad lessons or bad things that can happen to you and me; there is only good. Honestly, it took me a long time to understand and accept this lesson but the spirits are right. The good and the bad in life is all to be embraced and empower rather than weaken us. Life lessons (what we may consider bad things) are tough but should be lessons that help us grow and become full people.

Unfortunately, we do not learn without hardship. When things are going well and we are chugging along, we are not paying attention and are definitely not learning and growing as a soul. We are simply cruising along the road, enjoying the ride. When something goes wrong or we face a challenge along the road, we become who we really are. We fight, struggle, and hopefully overcome, never having to go through that lesson again. So we need to be grateful for hardship and move through it, leaving the crap (all the details and hurt) behind and taking the lesson forward with us. Does it really matter who did what and what mistakes were made? No. What's more important is how you dealt with it and moved through it. Details do not matter; the only thing that matters is what you got out of the experience.

Don't let your life lessons define you, let them be a small part of the whole you. Karma will take care of any wrongs people have done, so only worry about your own actions or lack of actions. And don't dwell on failure, because failure isn't when you try something that doesn't work out—failure is when you get knocked down and never get up again.

Spirit talks constantly about embracing the ebbs and flows of our lives and being grateful for both. When we do embrace them, not only do we allow ourselves to grow but we move more quickly to our big successes.

Fear

Fear is an illusion we create. Like happiness, it doesn't exist as a destination—it is a choice. For some of us, fears can actually be indicators of where our biggest successes lie. We need to learn to let go of fear, knowing it is something we have created that should never stop us. Instead, it should empower us to make needed changes. It really is true that "there is nothing to fear but fear itself." Once you learn to walk through your fears, you will be able to use them as tools with you controlling them rather than them controlling you. Did you know that fear of success is one of the most common fears out there? We may think fear of failure is most common, but most of us are quite familiar with failure; it is success we do not know—that unknown entity we desire but are afraid to grab because we don't know what will be involved or how it will really affect us. Our failures become like a safety blanket: we want out but cling to them out of fear of success. Until we realize our actual fear is not of failure, we will never walk forward.

Trust me when I say that I am walking, talking proof of the idea of fear of success. It has taken me a *long* time to complete this book. I've talked about having to write it to help people, and I'm constantly getting clients who are in desperate need of this book, but because of some bizarre fear (multiple fears, really) I have made every excuse there is when it came to completing it. I slowly pushed through those fears and made it happen because there is nothing better than walking through fear.

The situation with fear was very similar when it came to helping others in other ways, too. I was pushed and pulled into teaching classes by clients who wanted me to teach and help them. I wanted to help but was terrified because I was not someone who enjoyed standing in front of people speaking. I was driven to help my clients but swore I'd never ever do so much as a guided meditation. My mentor told me I had to, but in my rebellious ways I was completely opposed. When the day came for my first class, I was freaking out but was able to walk through the fear. And you know what? It went really well! I felt at least a little proud of myself.

One woman in the class really told me she needed to do meditation to learn how to relax outside of class. I decided that next week, I had to help her and do the meditation. The first meditation went well, and after a few weeks the ladies in my class asked me if there was any way I could record the meditation so they could do it at home. They said they had tried many different guided meditations but they didn't connect to them and really enjoyed mine. I was honored and shocked to say the least. What the experience taught me was that fear is a beacon—I needed to walk toward my fears to have the most success. Mind you, I'm not jumping out of an airplane anytime soon, but I'm open to walking through other fears.

There is No Try

"Do or do not—there is no try!" I hear this phrase a lot, and it is probably one of the biggest things many people need to learn. It's so simple but so complicated. One of my client's gatekeepers always puts it in a very simple way: it's a choice, plain and simple. You do something or you don't. Put that in your mouth or don't. Exercise or don't. You move forward or you don't. There is no try, so people need to forget the concept of "trying."

I am going to start a campaign in the near future to remove the word "try" from our language because there is *never* a good time to say it. Do not *try* to do something—do it or don't do it! It's a commitment. The spirits tell me that as humans, we basically give ourselves permission to sit on the fence by saying "try." "Oh, I'll try to lose weight," or "I'll try to change" but what we are really saying is "I can't do it right now, I'm not ready" or "I'm not going to commit." In one way or another, we are creating an excuse, and as my darling hubby says, "excuses are the road to failure."

Failure is *not* doing something but then it doesn't work out; failure is not an insufficient attempt or something that doesn't work out the way you wanted. It is when you don't fully commit and get stuck on your path feeling sorry for yourself. How many of us say "I'm going to try to lose weight" or "I'm going to try a certain diet this month" and then we stop? Maybe we get through one or two days—if you are really good, a week—and then when the results aren't what you think they should be, you quit. You say you "tried" and sure you did... *and* you didn't commit to doing it. You don't try to complete something or be the best at something—you *do* it!

A truly successful person in life is always doing. If something doesn't work out, they look at it as an opportunity, not a failure, and they *keep* doing. Remove "try" from your daily language because even by committing to *not* doing, you are still doing.

Let Go

Let go, and let God. This was a hard concept for me to understand at first because I always struggled with having a plan, moving forward with it, and then just letting go to let the universe make it happen. I thought: "Move forward but then let go? What? How does anyone do that?" After speaking to many dead people, I realize now this means that we need to walk our paths, be in the now, and do what we can to move forward, always working to be positive. While we are doing that, we need to let go of what we expect the destination will look like.

All too often, we limit our lives so much that we miss where we need to go. For example, imagine you are studying to be a lawyer and it is all you have ever wanted to be, but then something happens (the universe guides you) in your life that takes you toward being an advocate for children in the Third World. You may have needed information you learned on your path to being a lawyer that is also required to do your life's work, but it is not the destination that you imagined—it's better. Nothing in life is a waste of time or energy other than devoting both to fear and anger.

Everything happens for a reason, so we must trust and keep moving forward, letting the universe do its thing for us. This reasoning also applies to divinations and receiving messages. As I've explained before, messages are like a GPS for us but should never stop us from continuing to move forward. If you receive a message that you are going to meet the man of your dreams, but you decide to stay in the house and feel sorry for yourself because you have not met him yet, chances are he is not going to ring your doorbell and land in your lap. If you go out, work on yourself, and continue to live being the best and in the now, you will see and take opportunities that are presented to you. The universe will reward you for doing this and bring the right person to you... and chances are you'll meet that person when you least expect it.

On a weekly basis, I see the power of this trust. My husband always gets the best parking spot when we go shopping. He puts out the intention, "I'm going to get the best parking spot," trusts the universe to give it to him, and then he drives right to the spot waiting for him. This is manifesting (which is something else), but in order to successfully manifest anything, we need to let go and let God. Put out the intention, move toward it, work, and do what you can on your end, trusting and believing completely that the universe will supply the right outcome. With Steve and his parking spots, he completely can let go of the outcome—if he doesn't get the best spot, it isn't the end of the world. And if he stressed and grumbled about things, chances are he wouldn't get that spot. But he always gets the spot that is best for him just by letting go and letting the universe supply him with the perfect outcome.

Synchronicity

Synchronicity rules! Related to the last message of "let go and let God," it is the understanding that everything happens for a reason. You meet someone who introduces you to someone who gives you that job you have been wanting. Synchronicity often leaves me in awe when I think of the work the universe does, like how a thousand things had to happen to make one thing happen. With understanding synchronicity also comes the knowledge that success will happen when the time is right. If we push past the point of synchronicity because we are impatient and want to go from A to Z today instead of taking proper steps, the universe has to then line up another thousand things to make it happen at another point in the future.

Living in the now and being aware of opportunities and people around us is so important because when we are, we hit those marks on time if we follow the signs. The other thing about synchronicity is the knowledge that although we as humans love to think we are in control of our lives, we aren't. Sure, we have free will and can continue to ignore signs but then upheavals happen to make us pay attention. We can *still* continue to ignore the signs and go through life struggling, or we can take advantage of these opportunities the universe is presenting and improve our lives, like health issues for example. The only thing we do have complete control of is ourselves and our emotions: are we feeling positive or negative? Are we doing or "trying"? Realize that by doing, we meet synchronicity when we are meant to.

Buddhism speaks of a concept called the path of least resistance, which is about going with the flow and the balance between doing and allowing things to happen at the right time or being impatient and attempting to force something to happen. When we are impatient, we're not only not going with the flow, we set anchor and fight the currents so that nothing can move forward.

Many people don't even notice synchronicity or just brush it off, but on a daily basis it is happening. Gears are turning behind the scenes, like a clock or watch; we see the face but there are a lot of things happening behind it to make the hands move. The universe, our loved ones on the other side, and our guides are those gears, all working to connect the dots for us, putting people in our path or us in situations we need. Do you think when "coincidence" happens there isn't a bigger reason? Well, to let you in on a secret, there is no such thing as "coincidence."

Pay attention and you will see, from small things happening in life to big things, the gears are working to move you in the right direction. When we allow the gears to do their thing and go with the flow, we move faster and things tend to work out for the best. Again, it can be as small as going to purchase a new TV and the store you go to doesn't have the one you want. Maybe you'd freak out because you wanted that particular one so badly but you end up buying something else. If you went with the flow, chances are you'd leave, go to another store, and either get a better TV for the same money or the exact TV you wanted … on sale and with a surround sound system! The point is that the universe is always trying to help and support us, and synchronicity is the way they do it.

I'm reminded of a situation with one of my favorite clients. Before I met him, he was dating a woman for a few weeks who was also one of my clients. He had never really been to a medium but had a bunch of stuff going on, so she suggested he come see me. The following week after he visited, they broke up. I see her once a year, but he and I have become good friends, helping and supporting each other over the years. Synchronicity brought him to me not only to help him but also to bring a positive amazing person into my life. It took him meeting her through a few other people for her to bring him to me so we could aid each other at this stage of our lives.

There is something very important to know about synchronicity: if we push past the moment or sit and miss it, the universe *never* gives up. It will work and work to make another situation happen to connect the dots for us. So don't be stressed out if you miss an opportunity—another one will come around, though it may take some time for the universe to line up all the pieces again. Just remember that things may take longer to happen for you than you want if you don't go with the flow.

The Now

We often hear how we all need to live in "the now," and it is true. It is not healthy to live in the future, as there's no sense looking forward when we can't get past our fears today. If we don't live in the now, we will not make changes and grow to get to that awesome future.

It's okay to look a tiny bit forward but not much, as we need to stay in the now. It is equally important to stay out of the past—it is gone, and there is nothing you can do to change it, only build from it. In fact, the past is always happening—there it goes now! Every minute and second that passes is behind you, and you cannot do anything about it. Reminiscing about old times like the good old days of school or an embarrassing moment in your twenties is fun, but laughing and talking about these events does not help you now. The problem is people who tend to reminisce tend to live in the past. Unless you are a historian who is bringing the past into the now so we can learn from it, there is no need to spend time there. I'm not saying it isn't okay to get together with friends and have a laugh; it is completely okay but that's it—you cannot dwell back there. Likewise, any lessons we may have learned become a piece of us, but the details need to stay in the past.

When we live in the now, we see the signs and meet the people. Opportunity knocks and we actually hear it. We listen to synchronicity and go with the flow it provides. And in the now, we can be truly grateful for what's in front of us:

a wonderful meal, our kids and partner, friends, a beautiful flower, or a rain storm.

The more we are in the now, the more our ebbs and flows move. As a result, we move more quickly through them, getting to the empowered, full life we all want.

Positivity

Positivity is where it's at; we can all manifest things into our lives. Some people can be positive more easily than others, but every single one of us needs to remember this: thoughts have wings. Our thoughts take off and go out into the universe, so whatever we put out, we get back. If you wake up in the morning miserable, chances are the rest of your day will follow suit. If you are positive, the day will flow better. So if you are sending out need, you will get need back. If you are sending out anger and misery, you will get those back.

Many of us have heard of the law of attraction. This theory is right on, but in order to master it and manifest the Porsche in your driveway (if that's what you want) you need to master your thoughts. You must switch your thinking to be positive. We all have bad days and we're all just human, but the quicker you get off the pity party bus and jump on the happy train, the better your life will be.

Not only will being positive allow you to manifest amazing things into your life, but you will move quicker through the bad times (the ebbs) more easily. You will become grateful for them and realize that there is no such thing as bad times. All lessons are good; they lead us to a wonderful fulfilled life.

I AM!

This message is for those of us who can be (sort of) positive but can't lie to ourselves and fully commit to the law of attraction exercises.

Remember that our thoughts have wings, not our words. According to the law of attraction, you'd say something like "I have my shiny new Porsche in my driveway," but lots of people would then say in their head "I don't, really," which voids out the words. They say you need to fake it to make it, but I and many others have difficulty lying to ourselves.

One day, a dead person told me about "I AM," and thanks to synchronicity I turned on the TV that same day and saw Joel Osteen on *Oprah* speaking about the same thing! I love when that happens! The reasoning behind "I AM" is that whatever follows the words "I AM" will follow you. Does it work? Absolutely. It is simple and is not lying to yourself—it is what you want it to be.

Phrase your desires using I AM: "I AM attracting a Porsche to me"; "I AM facing fear"; "I AM doing"; "I AM attracting health and fitness into my life"; "I AM attracting the right people into my life"; "I AM attracting financial abundance." It sounds like a mantra or affirmation, but it is much more. Not only do you speak the words, you can easily and simply believe them too. There's no faking your mindset because it *is* your mindset.

As a quick hint, I sign my emails with my "I AM" affirmation—it is shocking how it works.

The Middle Way

The concept of the middle way or middle path has become popular via Buddhism, but I hear often from dead people that we all must try to work on following it. Due to our human nature and emotions, following this perfectly is nearly impossible. All we can do is work on keeping our emotions calm and as close to the middle way as possible, making it easier to move through life's ebbs and flows.

Think of the middle way as a normal day where nothing sets you off and nothing is overwhelmingly wonderful; you simply experience an average, ordinary day. Usually when something amazing happens to us and we are in a flow of life, our emotions sky rocket. After a few days up in the sky, we need to come back down to the norm, or the middle way. This realization leaves us feeling upset and down when really we are just at normal levels of being. Although nothing bad is happening, we aren't at that high any longer, so "normal" seems like a complete and utter bummer.

The same thing applies to an ebb: something bad happens, we drop below the middle way, and we have to claw and fight to come back to the norm. Many times, we analyze the ebb (bad thing) and wonder "Why me?" or think "Poor me, my life sucks." Thinking this way sinks that temporary drop even further below the middle, creating an even bigger hole to climb out of. Once we have finally climbed out of the hole and are back to normal, we are feeling fine about things but are exhausted from all the effort it took to get out of that hole.

What we need to work on is staying as close to the middle way as possible while still having our feelings, which we can do by not allowing our emotions to go to extremes. And the best way to do this is through gratitude. When something terrific happens, we celebrate and are grateful for it. Our emotions rise but do not jump to an extreme. When something negative happens, we are grateful for whatever the lesson is, knowing everything happens for a reason, even if we don't know the reason. We move through the difficulty back to the middle way with the knowledge that most ebbs are opportunities. This way, we are neither crashing after a high nor crawling out of the hole we created with our own upset and disappointment.

Following the middle path doesn't sound easy (and it isn't at times) but trust me—it is possible to train ourselves to do this. You *will* be in that flow I'm always talking about, and things will simply start to work out. You'll find yourself attracting more things and people to be grateful about, and that in turn will allow more to come to you.

Perspective

We must all realize that we all have our own realities, viewing things from our own unique perspectives. No one person sees a situation exactly as another person does. Even if two people see something similarly, they are not seeing it completely identically.

It sounds silly and obvious, but keep in mind: others are not you, and you are not them. No one can be you—only *you* can be you, and that's wonderful.

Studies have proven that if five people stand on a corner and witness an accident, all five of them see it differently. A few accounts may be similar, but no two are exactly alike. Knowing this prevents us from putting our expectations on others, letting us let go of harmful judgments like "I would *never* do that, why did they?" In most cases, other people are doing what they feel is right, acting just fine from their own perspective.

The way we see any given situation is not necessarily how others do. If you see the sky as blue and your friend sees it as orange, it doesn't matter. No matter how much you argue and try to prove your point, your friend will always see it as orange. Let go of the expectation that people should be you. You see the sky as blue and know it is blue to you, and you do not need to prove it to anyone. It is completely okay if your friend has their own beliefs. You can agree to disagree. Listen to other people's perspective and learn from them, but never expect others to understand our perspective.

When I think of the world's many religions, I definitely notice differences between faiths but see many more similarities. In many spiritualities, the message is the same but presented from different perspectives, different voices that speak the same core truths.

If we all started to accept differences, the world would change drastically. We could accept each other and not care so much about who is wrong and why—the truth is that we see the same thing, just a bit differently.

I've asked spirits several times why we all have different perspectives, and my guides told me that because all our souls are on different levels of evolution, we cannot practically understand certain elements of situations. If you are in grade one, you will look at things differently from someone who is in grade ten. And just because you may have had a hundred lives does not mean you are an old, evolved soul—you may have failed many grades and still be in grade one!

I now make an effort to always remember that we are all at different levels of soul evolution no matter what situation I'm in. I understand that I do not need to prove my perspective to someone who doesn't want to hear it or learn from it. None of us can put our expectations on anyone else.

Graveyards

A lot of people ask me about graveyards and gravesites. They want to know: are they haunted? And are dead people lingering there with their bodies? Some graveyards are haunted but not as many as you think, and ghosts can sometimes be attached to their bodies or to the land. If a ghost is stuck and grabs on to what it knows, it may stick with its body or a familiar landmass, but it's more common for them to go to a home or location where they lived or died. Unless the ghost was killed in the graveyard, chances are they'd be elsewhere, so graveyards are really not that scary. Likewise, spirits are not at their gravesites all the time, only when they follow us to the site. So, you do not need to go to a gravesite to connect to the dead.

Even though ghosts and spirits do not typically linger around gravesites and memorial sites, they are important places because they offer us, the living, a special space of contemplation to connect with loved ones. Gravesites are also ways we can honor and respect our loved ones' lives; after the body is laid to rest in whatever manner the family feels is appropriate, the spirit can then move forward and be at peace. Every so often, I'll go to someone's house to do a clearing and will see an urn on the mantle. When I question the homeowner, they will inform me the urn contains the remains of a loved one who passed away a few years prior. Although I understand the need to keep it, it does not help the dead person or the living move on from the death.

There are occasions when I have seen that if the dead person has not crossed over, it can cause them to be stuck until their ashes are put to rest.

Glossary

Akashic records: A place where books holding the entire stories of our soul's journey is kept. Past lives, lessons learned and not learned, current life, future lessons, emotions, thoughts, and intent are kept here.

Automatic writing: A form of trance channeling that allows Spirit to use your arm and hand to write a message from the other side.

Chakras: The main energy sources in your body. There are seven main chakras: root, sacral, solar plexus, heart, throat, third eye, and crown.

Clairaudience: Clear hearing. The ability to hear with the spiritual ear. There are two types of clairaudience: subjective and objective.

Clairgustance: A form of spirit communication that uses the sense of taste. The ability to smell odors no one else can smell will help identify the spirit present.

Clairsentience: The most common form of spirit communication, this refers to a sense of feeling or knowingness. Clairsentience does not involve visualization or mental images of any kind; you simply sense or feel something. Often called intuition or a gut feeling.

Clairvoyance: Clear seeing, or the ability to see with the spiritual mind's eye (often called the third eye). You may see images, pictures, symbols, and even colors. There are two types of clairvoyance: subjective and objective.

Cleansing: The practice of cleaning the energy in or around a person, place, or item.

Clearing: Removing entities, ghosts, or spirits from a location.

Cords or cords of attachment: These are energy cords that are often attached to you from another person sending you energy; many times, these cords are negative. Negative cords should be removed because they can affect your energy and moods, making you feel ill or off. These cords can be removed through meditation or reiki.

Dead time: Between 3 and 4 am, the period of time in which spirit energy is the highest and the veil to the other side is especially thin.

Developmental meditation: A form of meditation that helps develop psychic abilities.

Divination: The practice of using tools to connect and gain insight in the metaphysical world.

Dogma: A doctrine or body of doctrines concerning faith or morals formally stated and authoritatively proclaimed by a religious authority.

Dowsing: Also known as divining or water witching. Dowsing is a type of divination used to locate water, items, people, and Spirit. It is also used to ask direct questions to spirits via yes or no questions.

EMF or electromagnetic field meter: This device is used to detect unexplained fluctuations in electromagnetic frequencies. Because spirit and ghosts are mostly energy, they can be located with one of these meters. These meters are also helpful in debunking hauntings, giving the user the ability to see if there is a physical reason for the fluctuation such as a plug that is not grounded properly or electrical lines in a location giving off a large amount of EMF. This may cause a person to feel stressed and anxious, and even sometimes paranoid.

Empath: A person who feels other people's emotions, aliments, and energy. They also feel the energy from Spirit and items.

EVP or electronic voice phenomena: The picking up of spirit voices on a recording device.

Flame cards: A method of divination that uses a blank recipe card and a candle. The card is held and your energy is put in it. The card is then briefly passed over the flame of a candle, which leaves a design or image on the card. Inspect the card to see what the picture reveals; many times, you will see a person or symbol. Also remember to hold your hand over the card, taking care to not touch the picture or it will smudge. Feel the energy coming off the card.

Guides: Souls on the other side that are from past lives that are here to guide you to learn your lessons. We all have our own guides and entourage. There are inner band and outer band guides. Inner guides are not shared, and outer band guides come in to help us with specific things, such as reiki or tarot.

Karma: Karma is created by how we treat others and our intent with our actions. Always remember what you put out is what you get back—some people say tenfold or a hundredfold. Karma is governed by the universe. Cause and effect.

Medium: A person who has the ability to communicate with the dead.

Objective clairaudience: The ability to hear the dead as if it is coming through the physical ear.

Objective clairvoyance: The ability to see psychic visions in the same way as with the physical eyes. Symbols can also be seen in this way.

Pendulum: A form of divination. A pendulum is a weight suspended from a pivot so it can swing freely. It can be a crystal or metal hanging from a chain. Many people in the past would use a ring on a necklace.

Poltergeist: German for "noisy ghost." Poltergeists are a type of ghost or supernatural entity responsible for physical disturbances. As things have evolved in the metaphysical world, a poltergeist is more about the type of activity rather than the spirit itself. Others refer to poltergeists as the manifestations of spirits of the lowest level, i.e., malicious spirits.

Psychometry: A divination used by a person who has the ability to feel and/or see information by holding an item. This can also be used to help a medium connect to a soul on the other side, bringing them forward to communicate.

Reiki: A Japanese form of healing using energy.

Remote viewing: The ability to travel to a person or location while awake. Remote viewing allows a viewer to see and feel what is happening in the location.

Runes: An ancient Germanic alphabet, used for writing, divination, and magic. They were used throughout northern Europe, Scandinavia, and Iceland from about 100 BCE. Using rune casting, runes are an oracle form which one may seek advice. Runes are most often made of wood or stone.

Scrying: A divination using an item to receive messages; most common are a crystal ball, mirror, or a glass/bowl of water.

Semi-trance: In this state, the medium is aware of what is going on and knows they are being used as a channel. The medium is usually strongly impressed with the personality of the spirit but is still in control of their body and voice.

Subjective clairaudience: Similar to mental telepathy or thought transference, you hear the thought as if it is spoken in your mind.

Subjective clairvoyance: Spirit impresses mental pictures upon the mind that may be images of things past, present, or future. A message may also come across as symbols the medium has to interpret.

Tarot: Divination using cards. Tarot can be performed using simple playing cards, or various decks in a nearly endless variety of art styles.

Trance: The simple definition is that the consciousness of the medium no longer functions on the material plane, leaving the physical body open to channel. The spirit uses the medium's body and voice to communicate. The medium is not aware of what is happening.

Witching hour (*See* **Dead time**): The time of the day when the dead are said to be the most active and the veil to the other side at its thinnest. Between 3 am and 4 am.